Flower Delights

Flower Delights

40 Enjoyable Things to Do with Flowers

Illustrations by **Sara Princé**
Text by **Sandrine Tournigand**

CONTENTS

FLOWER FACTS

FLORAL INSPIRATION

FLOWER KNOWLEDGE

CONTENTS

FLOWERY STORIES

FLORAL TREATS

MORE INFORMATION

Introduction

Beautiful, delicate, powerful, bewitching, ephemeral—flowers color our lives and make us feel good; it's proven! More than ever, they are the symbol of a creative and ultrafresh rebirth.

Whatever the civilization, flowers have seduced artists, writers, painters, and fashion designers.

No one can ignore the infinite diversity of their shapes and colors, their mystery, their symbolic power, their medicinal virtues. Ephemeral, sometimes immortal, delicate, and powerful at the same time, cultivated or wild, mute or fragrant, magical or aphrodisiac, flowers fascinate, perfume, charm, heal, and bewitch.

Designed like a bouquet of flowers where botany, floral stories, floral know-how, and floral recipes merge happily, this feel-good book offers an inspiring and inspired escape, an explosion of flowers that we love to browse through.

Throughout this book, we have sown garlands of flowers, flower paintings, boutonnieres, potpourri, centerpieces, and scented waters, and recipes for herbal teas or flower drinks that you can use as inspiration for your floral creations or to give as gifts, or just to make you smile.

All this is accompanied by eighty pages of floral stationery: Kraft paper, planters, postcards, origami paper, bookmarks, gift tags, coasters, and stickers to give a boost to your creations.

Like a bursting seedpod, spread flowers all around you!

Sara Princé and Sandrine Tournigand

WHO'S WHO

THE ANEMONE, FLOWER OF THE WIND

What is it?

With its large black-hearted flowers, the anemone is easily recognizable. Similar to the poppy, the anemone takes its name from the Greek word ***anemos***, which means "wind." It owes this name to the feathery seeds that the slightest breeze carries away: it's the flower of the wind! Also, Greek mythology tells that the god of the winds, Zephyr, fell in love with a nymph named Anemone, and out of jealousy, her husband turned her into a flower and took away all her fragrance. In 1640, the botanist Bachelier brought back from Constantinople the first anemone seeds that he secretly germinated in his Parisian garden. Two centuries later, there were more than a thousand varieties of anemones in a multitude of colors; they inspired Guillame Apollinaire to write his famous poem "Clotilde."

What is its symbolism?

In a bouquet, the anemone, a symbol of sincerity, sends the desperate message "I don't want to lose you!"

How does it fit in a bouquet?

You can create a bouquet with anemones of different colors. To give it volume, add ferns or bear grass, foliage with long, threadlike leaves. Anemones also go very well with pink-fuchsia ranunculus, roses, blue thistles, and hyacinths.

How do you maintain it?

If it's not too hot, prepare the anemones to enjoy them for at least a week: cut the stems a few centimeters long and dip the ends in boiling water for thirty seconds . Then place them in a vase filled with lukewarm water. The stems of the anemones bend in the light. Arrange your bouquet in a place with subdued light. Both anemones and tulips continue to grow even when cut.

PISTILS
The anemone has a forest of pistils at its center.

THE CHALICE
It consists of five to eight free, petal-like sepals.

SEPALS
This flower is said to be incomplete, since it has sepals instead of petals.

LEAVES
They are generally dark green and highly prized for their decorative appearance.

STAMENS
A crown of black stamens contrasts with the bright colors of the flower.

STEM
It can measure between 16 and 24 inches.

COLORS
White, purple, red, or purplish blue, anemones have shimmering colors.

FLOWERY WORDS

From time immemorial, the beauty of flowers has never ceased to inspire writers, artists, poets, and philosophers. Here are some selected pieces of the most-beautiful flower quotations.

If you love a flower that lives in a star, it's sweet to look at the sky at night.

Antoine de Saint-Exupéry

Love is like the wild rose-briar,
Friendship like the holly-tree—
The holly is dark when the rose-briar blooms
But which will bloom most constantly?

Emily Bronte

If life is but a passage, on that passage let us at least sow flowers.

Michel de Montaigne

There are flowers everywhere for anyone who wants to see them.

Henri Matisse

The Butterfly. This love letter, folded in two, is looking for a flowery address.

Jules Renard

Life is a flower. Love is its honey.

Victor Hugo

Use the labels in this book to add a sweet note to your bouquet.

FLORA-THERAPY

38 Flower Elixirs from Dr. Bach®

Managing your emotions with flowers is possible with flora-therapy. Although the effectiveness of flowers on our behavior has not yet been scientifically proven, this alternative medicine, which has been practiced for nearly a century, has many followers. Bach® flowers take their name from their inventor: Dr. Edward Bach. In the 1930s, this British doctor specialized in bacteriology and, as a supporter of homeopathy, began to develop herbal elixirs. His idea was that emotions and personality traits disrupted what he called the "flow of life," leading to physical dysfunction.

According to him, to cure diseases, we must first act on emotions. For this very religious man, a remedy cannot be found anywhere else but in Nature created by God. He postulated that flowers contain the "quintessence" of healing virtues of a plant and drew up a sort of table listing the properties of thirty-eight flower or plant essences. Each one has an effect on our moods: honeysuckle for nostalgia, larch for lack of confidence, gentian when you are discouraged, etc. Bach's final elixir is called Rescue®, a mixture of five flowers. The flower elixir is taken orally by pouring a few drops into a glass of water.

GENTIAN

Sometimes grown in gardens, it's primarily a wild plant. Its deep, intense blue flowers are an eye-catcher on mountain paths. With its long tubular corolla, the shape of the gentian is also very special, since it looks like a trumpet. It's the Bach® flower of perseverance. With it, nothing is insurmountable.

HELIANTHEMUM

The helianthemum, whose Greek name means "flower of the sun," has very delicate yellow flowers. They bloom only in full sunlight and rarely last more than a day. Also very fragile, the petals fall off when touched. However, this plant is much stronger than it looks, since it manages to bloom under difficult conditions. Helianthus soothes and gives courage and hope.

WILD ROSE

The Romans used the root of this wild rose to treat rabies; hence its nickname, "dog rose." At the end of its abundant flowering, the rose hip produces rose hips. These small red and oval balls have a sweet and tangy taste with a fruity note and are very rich in vitamin C. The wild rose is the Bach® flower of joy and dynamism.

FLOWERY STORIES

Liberty Print

Englishman Arthur Lasenby Liberty gave his name to this flowery print. In 1875, this globetrotter—who was in love with colors and Asian products—opened a fabric store on Regent Street in London, which he named Liberty of London. He sold all kinds of goods imported from the East: Chinese porcelain and silk, Indian fabrics, Japanese fans. The shop was a great success and grew rapidly.

However, Arthur Liberty, disappointed over the years with the quality of the Asian textiles received, decided to use local manufacturers to design his own printed fabrics. In 1884, he imagined a fine cotton fabric decorated with delicate floral motifs visible on both sides of the fabric, and Liberty was born. In order to diversify his motifs, Arthur Liberty surrounded himself with the most-eminent creators, including the Arts & Crafts artist Lindsay P. Butterfield. The businessman also participated in the development of art nouveau, to the point that in Italy, this artistic movement is called "stile Liberty" or "floreale."

THE LIBERTY SCARF: A "MUST-HAVE"

In the 1950s, the Liberty scarf was in the wardrobe of every English woman. This little silk square allowed you to play with prints and add a touch of color and sparkle to an outfit without the risk of bad taste. Queen Elizabeth II loves these flowery fabrics. Today, an accessories department launches new designs every season and reinterprets archival designs.

CACHAREL CONTRIBUTED TO ITS GLORY

In 1900, the Liberty brand opened a Parisian branch. Paul Poiret used the floral fabric for his creations. Then, in the 1960s, Yves Saint Laurent succumbed to the romanticism of prints. But it was mainly Cacharel who made Liberty known in France. At the end of the 1960s, designer Jean Bousquet democratized printing with his famous floral blouse, which became the brand's bestseller. A panoply of models followed, including tank tops, dresses, skirts, bikinis, shorts, headbands, and smock dresses. At that time, Cacharel bought nearly a million meters of Liberty cloth a year.

FLOWER YOUR JAM JARS

MATERIALS

- Jam jar
- Liberty fabric remnant
- Pink ribbon
- Tailor's chalk
- Pair of pinking shears
- White vinyl glue

HOW TO

Place the lid of the jam jar on the Liberty cloth. Draw a chalk circle around the lid, leaving a margin of at least an inch. Cut out the circle of fabric with scissors. Spread the glue on it and place it in the center of the lid. Fold down the edges, place the lid on the jar, and tie the ribbon to form a collar.

RECIPE

DANDELION FLOWER JAM

INGREDIENTS

- 7 oz. dandelion flowers
- Water
- 3 oranges
- 3 lemons
- 2 lb. granulated sugar

Remove the petals. Spread them out in a crate for two hours to let any trapped insects escape.

Pour 1 quart of water into a saucepan and add the petals. Add the sliced oranges and lemons. Bring to the boil and then simmer for one hour.

Filter the juice, then weigh it. Add the equivalent of this weight in sugar and bring to the boil. Continue cooking for forty-five minutes, skimming regularly.

As soon as the jam starts to thicken, put it into jars. Flip the filled jars over to prevent mold from forming.

Decorate your jam jars with the pretty flower labels from this book.

RECIPE

ROSE JAM

INGREDIENTS

- 18 oz. untreated rose petals
- 35 oz. granulated sugar for jam
- 3 tablespoons rose water
- 4 oz. slivered almonds

Place the rose petals in a bowl with 1 cup of cold water and leave to macerate for twelve hours. Then drain the petals and pour the maceration water and the sugar into a saucepan.

Heat while stirring, bring to a simmer, skim, and add the petals to this syrup. Add the rose water and continue cooking five minutes at low boiling until the jam thickens.

Add the almonds and leave to stand for ten minutes. Bring to a boil again, stir a final time, and put the jam into jars. Flip the filled jars over to prevent mold.

Decorate your jam jars with the pretty flower labels from this book.

THE TULIP, EMBLEM OF THE NETHERLANDS

What is it?

Hardly anything is more Dutch than the tulip, and yet this flower that grows wild at the foot of the Himalayas had its first success in the Ottoman Empire.

In Constantinople, the sultans had a real cult for it, and its name comes from the Turkish word ***tülbent***, which means "turban." Like the headdress, the flower can have a multitude of shapes and colors. The first bulbs were imported to Vienna in the sixteenth century by the Austrian ambassador in office in the time of Suleiman the Magnificent. However, it was the Dutch who became passionate about this exotic flower. The bulb trade became speculative, leading to the notorious "tulip mania." Some extremely rare species could reach 10,000 guilders, the price of a house with a garden and stable near the canals of Amsterdam! No other flower has been so valuable. Holland remains the world's largest producer of tulips.

What is its symbolism?

The tulip generally symbolizes love, with nuances that vary according to its color: a yellow tulip expresses despair in love, while a red tulip expresses eternal love and mad passion. The rarer the color of the flower, the more the person who offers it proves they're willing to ruin themselves for the one they love.

How does it fit in a bouquet?

There is such a choice of colors and shapes that a simple bunch of tulips is beautiful. Mixing double-flowered varieties with the more slender lily varieties will be most effective. A bouquet of roses, carnations, eucalyptus, and tulips? Bliss!

How do you maintain it?

These flowers appreciate the cold. Add a few ice cubes in water for a night on a balcony to give them tone and rigidity. Unlike other flowers, even when cut, they continue to grow. Put them in a vase filled with only 4 inches of water. To stimulate the buds to open, prick the stem just below the flower with a pin. Air will be able to escape, which will facilitate the passage of water.

THE PETALS

The tulip has six. If the contours are jagged and ragged, it's a parrot tulip. When tapered to the tip, it's a lily tulip.

STEM

Supple and can measure between 8 and 24 inches.

LEAVES

Smooth, they have the appearance of a narrow lance. They are said to be lanceolate.

COLORS

It exists in white, red, yellow, orange, pink, purple, and green. Black tulips are the dream of all horticulturists and also the muse of writers.

THE BULB

Tulip bulbs are planted in the garden in the fall.

FLORAL PLAYLIST

To the rhythm of these famous French songs, let yourself be lulled by stories of flowers and love.

My Friend the Rose

We're very few things.
And my friend the rose told me that this morning
At dawn I was born, baptized with dew,
I blossomed happy and in love.

Françoise Hardy

The Power of Flowers

Change the world, change things with bouquets of roses. Change women, change men with geraniums.

Laurent Voulzy

A Pretty Flower

A pretty flower in the guise of a bitch, a pretty bitch disguised as a flower, who flaunts her beauty and ties you up, then leads you by your heartstrings.

Georges Brassens

Flowers

Inside every man lives the seed of a flower. If he looks within he finds beauty and power. Ring all the bells sing and tell the people that be everywhere that the flower has come.

Minnie Riperton

Flower Time

It was the time of flowers, we ignored fear, the tomorrows tasted like honey.

Dalida

Seasonal Flower

I smell like lilies. My muscles are restrengthening. And I'm waiting for the flowering. But what the hell happened between September and May. I've forgotten my name.

Émilie Simon

Eat Flowers

He liked to eat flowers
So they grew in his stomach
And meadows full of color
Covered his heart in his lair.
He liked to eat the flowers.
It was his secret garden.
Clarika

Flowers

I think of the flowers, which are
perfect, which have no other role
than to exist.
Clara Luciani

The Flower

I loved a flower, she taught me love,
she taught me how to cry. It was so natural.
I was so polluted. She was so
beautiful. I liked to smell her.
Mathieu Chedid

HERBAL TEAS

Flower Infusions

Drinking herbal tea in the evening is a moment of pure pleasure, but it also helps you to relax before sinking into the arms of Morpheus. Everyone can invent their own mixture. Depending on the flowers used, an infusion can be refreshing or wintery, relaxing or aphrodisiac, soothing or energizing. In fact, every flower has its benefits. Marjoram is effective against anxiety, lavender brings serenity, mint is tonic and stimulating. Valerian, lavender, or chamomile soothes and facilitates sleep; linden flowers calm coughing; mallow helps concentration; dog rose is recommended for circulation problems. Contrary to what one might believe, the active ingredients are often extracted more easily from dried plants. But the freshly picked plants often make tastier herbal teas.

Beyond their medicinal virtues, flowers are also used for their decorative aspect. Poppy and dog rose, with their red colors, can stimulate, warm, and excite. Orange marigold flowers and yellow sunflowers put people in a good mood and bring joy to life. Cornflowers and lavender, in mauve and blue hues, calm the spirits. With your herbal tea ready, add a little sweetness with a spoonful of honey, especially if bees have foraged the flower that corresponds to your tea.

CUSTOMIZE YOUR HERBAL TEA CANISTER

MATERIALS

- A sheet of origami paper found in this book
- Glue
- Fine paintbrush
- A ruler
- Measuring tape
- Pencil

HOW TO

Use a flexible tape measure to measure the rounded surfaces of your herbal tea can to reproduce the shape on the sheet of paper. Cut it out carefully. Apply glue to the reverse side of the paper and smooth it out so that air bubbles are removed. Leave it to dry.

CHAMOMILE

Taken as an infusion in the evening, the chamomile flower helps you sleep. It has calming and digestive virtues. Matricaria chamomile is appreciated for its scent, which evokes sour apples. Its name comes from a Greek expression meaning "apple of the sky." Its aroma is sweeter than that of Roman chamomile.

ORANGE BLOSSOM

Orange blossom smells like the Mediterranean. It does not come from orange trees but from bitter orange trees. Appreciated for its taste and delicate fragrance, it symbolizes maternal caress and calms anxiety and stress. Its leaves and beautiful white flowers have a sedative and relaxing effect. For an herbal tea, boil 1–2 teaspoons of dried flowers in 7 fluid ounces of water. Taste it half an hour before bedtime.

LINDEN

Deliciously fragrant, the linden flower is rich in flavonoids (antioxidants). As an infusion, it soothes and helps you sleep. Its action on sleep disorders is not new. In the past, it was customary to give children who were too agitated in the evening a bath in linden-infused water.

VAN GOGH'S SUNFLOWERS

In 1888, while living in Arles, in the south of France, Vincent van Gogh prepared for a visit by Paul Gauguin. To decorate his friend's room, he painted bouquets of sunflowers, because this flower symbolizes respect, admiration, and friendship: it follows the sun all day long, as if to contemplate it. Like the artist, it can live only in the light, and like the sun, the work created by the painter provides light and nourishes the soul. The result was a series of seven paintings showing the evolution of sunflowers, from blooming to withering, as a metaphor for life passing by.

RECORD-BREAKING AUCTIONS

In 1891, the writer Octave Mirbeau bought one of the copies from Father Tanguy for 300 francs (900 euros). In 1987, at an auction at Christie's in London, Yasuo Goto, a tycoon from the insurance industry in Japan, acquired a painting of the series for the equivalent of 40.8 million euros! The price was judged scandalous by Jean Ferrat, who wrote the song *Les Tournesols*, where he evokes the wretched life of the painter. A few months later, more than 2,200 art enthusiasts from all over the world were present at the auction at Sotheby's of Vincent van Gogh's painting ***Irises***. The painting fetched the incredible sum of $53.9 million. In five years, the impressionists' popularity has increased fourfold, and Van Gogh's has increased eightfold.

ONLY SIX SUNFLOWERS

Of these seven works, only six remain today. One was destroyed in a fire when the American army bombed the Japanese city of Ashiya in 1945. The sunflowers are now in museums around the world: Amsterdam, London, Munich, Tokyo, and Philadelphia, and in a private collection in the United States. None of them are ever exhibited elsewhere because they are considered too fragile to be transported.

FLORAL DRINKS

POPPY CORDIAL

INGREDIENTS

for 8.5 fluid ounces of cordial

- The petals of 25 poppies
- 2 lemons
- 2 oz. sugar
- 10 fluid oz. water

Dissolve the sugar in water heated on the stove. Add half of the poppies and the lemon juice. Simmer for ten minutes, remove from the heat, and add the rest of the poppies. Leave to cool for about three hours, filter, and pour it into a bottle.

Like the opium poppy, of which it's a close cousin, the poppy contains alkaloids responsible for its calming properties.

To decorate your bottle of poppy cordial, use the stickers in this book.

FLOWER ICE CUBES

INGREDIENTS

You can safely use lavender, violet, wisteria, cornflower, nasturtium, lilac, chamomile, and rose. You can also add aromatic herbs (thyme, rosemary, verbena, mint), fruit (blackberries, blueberries, currants, raspberries), or agave syrup for sweet and fragrant ice cubes.

HOW TO

Remove each stem so that only the flower remains.

Rinse the flowers with water.

Distribute the flowers in each compartment of an ice cube tray.

Pour water halfway up and place the tray in the freezer.

Top off the compartments with water four hours later, so that the fruit or herb will be properly caught inside the ice cube, since it might float on the surface at the beginning of the freezing process. Put the ice cube tray back in the freezer and wait for the magic of the cold to work.

WHO'S WHO

THE ROSE, QUEEN OF FLOWERS

What is it?

According to Greek mythology, this flower was white until Aphrodite dyed the petals with her blood as she tried to rescue Adonis, her wounded lover. Scientists believe it has been around for nearly thirty-five million years. In ancient times, the rose was proclaimed queen of flowers and charmed the Greeks, Romans, and Egyptians. There are also traces of its cultivation in China and Persia 5,000 years ago. During the crusades in the eleventh century, new species were imported to Europe, including the famous Damask rose, which is so fragrant. Over the centuries, it became the muse of poets and the star of gardens. Today, the French Rose Society, founded in Lyon in 1886, lists more than 40,000 varieties of roses.

What is its symbolism?

It's the most romantic flower. The red rose is associated with passionate love, while the white expresses the sincerity of feelings. In addition to its color, the number that one offers is also rich in symbolism: one rose to reveal one's love in all simplicity; two to make amends; twelve when proposing.

How does it fit in a bouquet?

There is such a variety of species and colors that any flower can be associated with its queen: lisianthus, astrantia, thistle, sea lavender, dahlia, cosmos, hellebore, ranunculus, and gypsophila. A few eucalyptus leaves elegantly decorate a bouquet.

How do you maintain it?

For better water absorption, cut the stems at a 45° angle, ideally under a trickle of water, with good pruning shears. Leave the thorns and remove the leaves that are below the water level. To give a second life to your bouquet, plant a stem in a potato and you will obtain a rose bush for the garden.

THE PETALS

The cultivated rose has a myriad of interlocking petals, while the wild rose has only five petals.

STEM

Rigid, it has thorns. This means of defense is also a temperature regulator.

COLORS

It can be pink, white, red, orange, yellow, blue, and sometimes even mixed or bicolor.

PIERRE DE RONSARD AND THE ROSE

My sweet, let us see whether the rose for Cassandra

My sweet, let us see whether the rose
which this morning had opened
its purple dress in the sun
has retained this evening
the folds of its purple dress,
and its complexion so akin to yours.

Alas! See in how little time,
my sweet, it let fall, alas,
its beauty on the ground!
Oh, nature, cruel mother,
for such a flower only lasts
from dawn until dusk!

So, if you believe me, my sweet,
while your age is blossoming
in its greenest form,
gather, gather your youth:
as with this flower, old age
will tarnish your beauty.

Pierre de Ronsard
"Ode to Cassandra," 1550

On April 21, 1545, Pierre de Ronsard fell in love at first sight. During a ball at Blois Castle, he met Cassandre Salviati, descendant of a noble Florentine family. She was only fifteen years old, and he was twenty-one. She was so beautiful, and her eyes were so sweet, that the poet fell madly in love with her. It was an impossible love that ended the following year when the beautiful Cassandra married someone else. However, this platonic love inspired Ronsard to write one of his most famous odes, "My sweet, let us see whether the rose," where he compares her to the queen of flowers.

Use the postcards in this book to send a poem to the person you love.

Pierre de Ronsard

Ode à Cassandre

1550

FLORAL WATERS

Beauty Secrets

Delicately scented floral waters and hydrolytes are a treasure trove of benefits in cosmetics. Hydrolyte water is a distillation of the whole or partial plant (leaves, branches, twigs, roots), while floral water results from the distillation of the flowering top. Originally, these waters were created to trap the scents of aromatic plants. Collected at the distillation stage, they convey the subtle message of plants and essential oils. When they come out of the still, they correspond to the water vapor, which condenses as it cools and then separates from the essential oil. During distillation, these waters are loaded with aromatic molecules, incorporating, incidentally, a small part of the principal plant's active ingredients. Their use is therefore also therapeutic. Much less concentrated than essential oil (from 0.05% to 0.1% aromatic molecules), these colored waters are particularly soft and well tolerated, which allows them to be used on the face, eyes, body, or hair without fear of irritation. There are dozens of variations: black currant, cinnamon, lemongrass, mint, basil, elderberry, ylang-ylang, rosemary, Damask rose, lavender, lemon balm, neroli.

MAKE YOUR OWN ROSE WATER

INGREDIENTS

- 6 gallons mineral water
- 3.5 oz. rose petals

HOW TO

Boil the mineral water and add the petals. Let it steep for twelve hours. Filter the preparation and conserve it in an airtight sterile bottle.

Decorate your rose water bottle with one of the labels in this book.

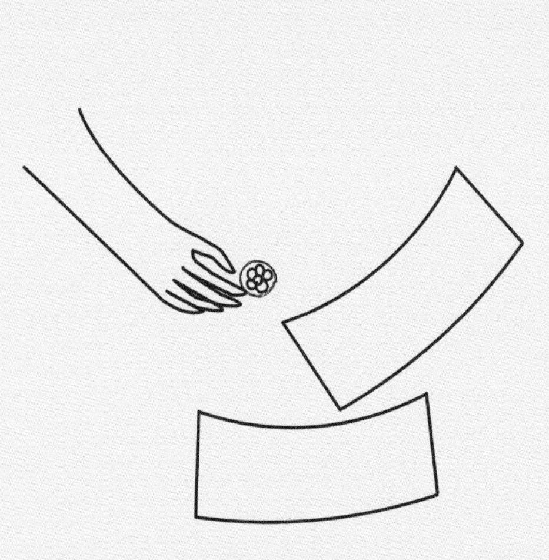

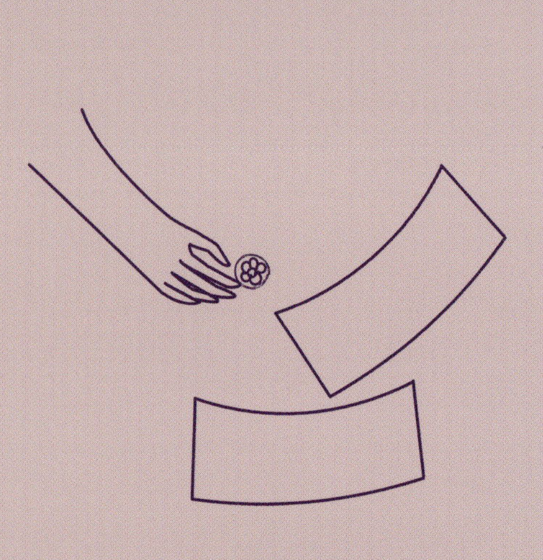

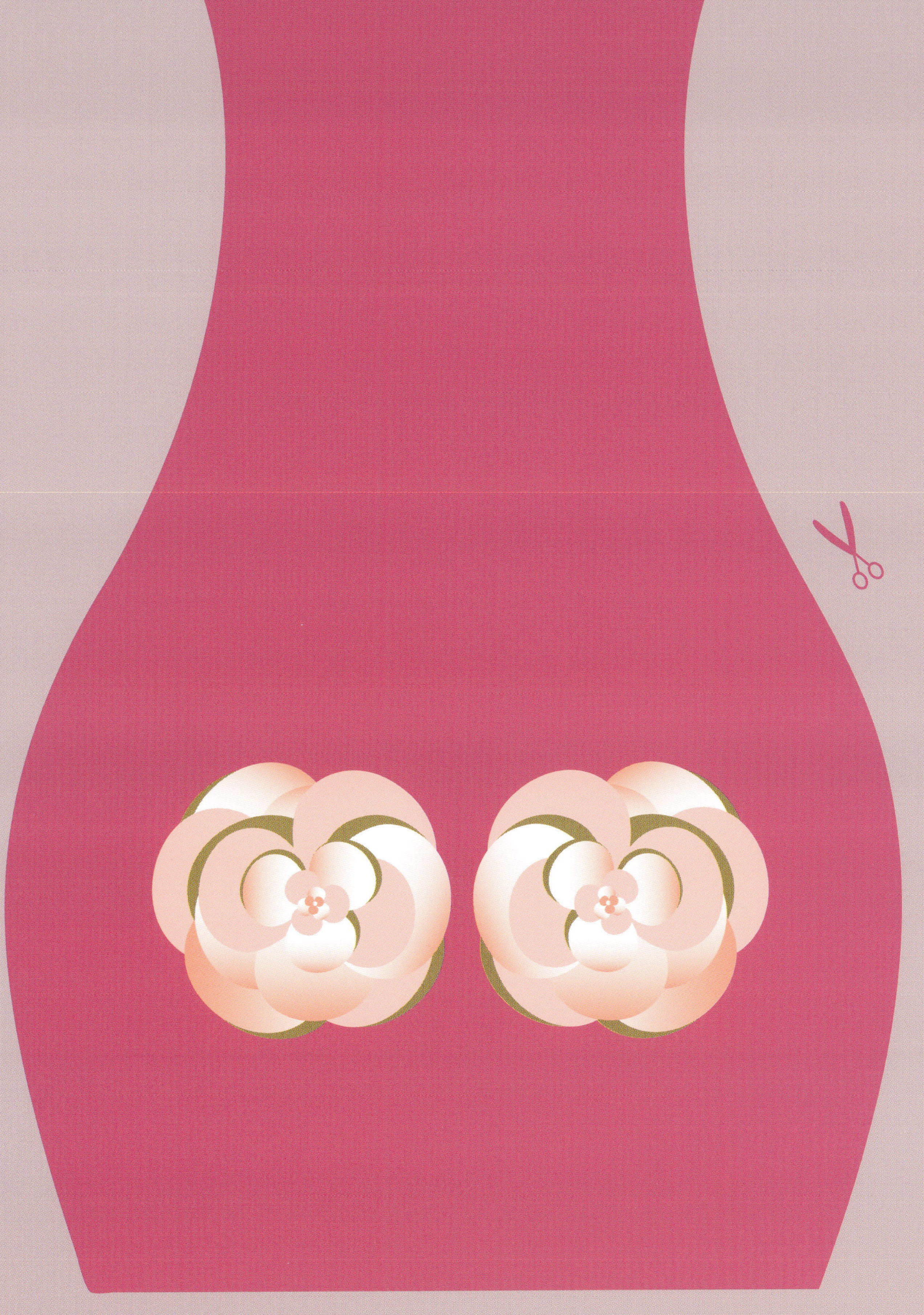

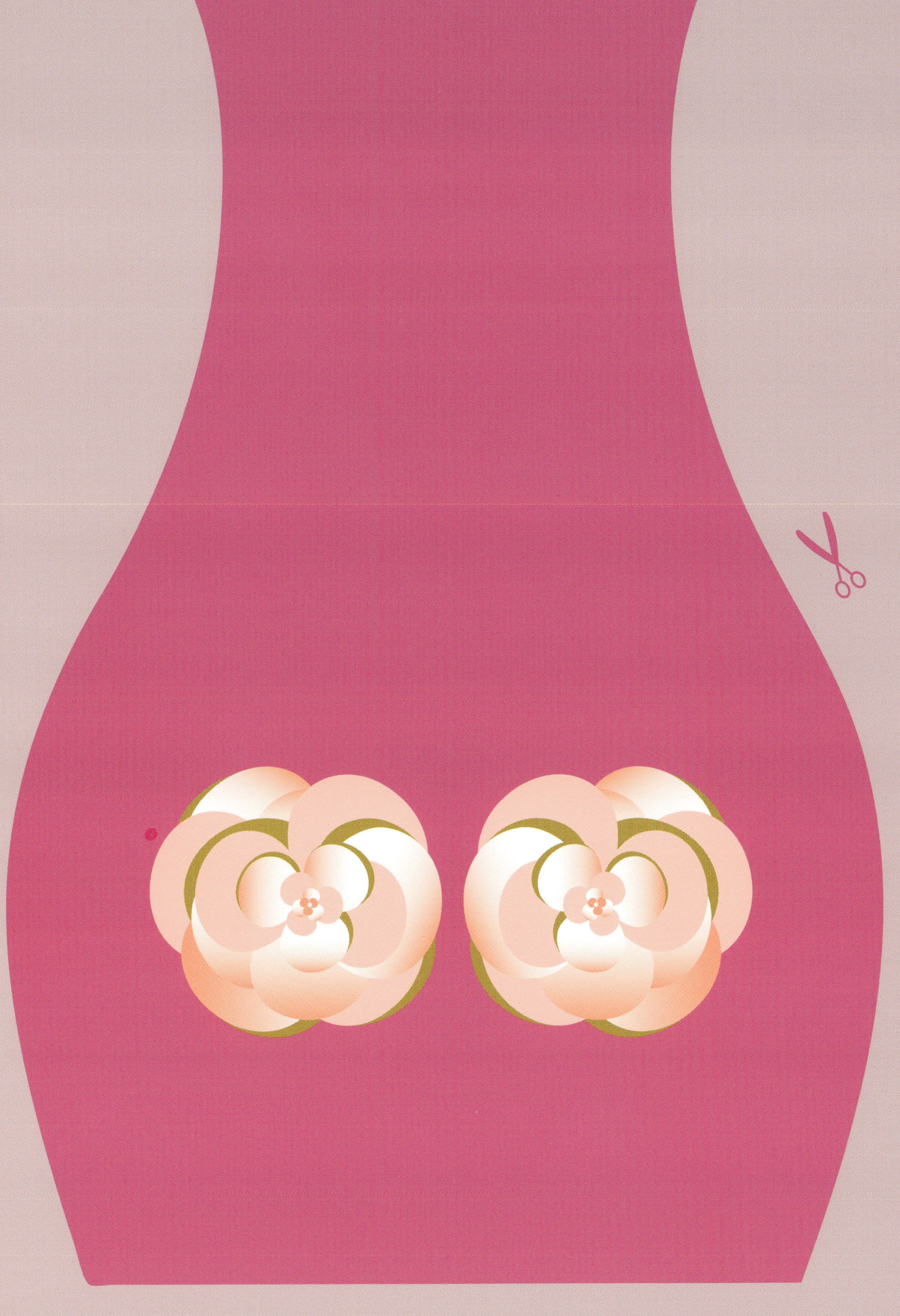

CORNFLOWER

Contrary to legend, cornflowers do not enhance the color of blue eyes. On the other hand, the flower is reputed to relieve irritated eyes and reduce swelling in eyelids. In the Middle Ages, those who rubbed their face with it were protected from eye diseases.

ROSE

Delicate and feminine, the Damask rose (*Rosa damascena*) and the May rose (*Rosa centifolia*) are known for their softness and cosmetic active ingredients. Rose hydrolyte is ideal for waking the skin in the morning and beautifying the complexion. Rose water can also be used as a home fragrance. With its sweet and voluptuous scent, it also relaxes the mind and relieves anxiety.

LAVENDER

Already known in Roman times for its purifying properties, lavender—from the Latin *lavare* (to wash)—was used to perfume baths and laundry. Lavender floral water cleanses and softens the skin and scalp. Redness, itching, sunburn, and other skin irritations are no match for it. Eau de Cologne, created in the town of the same name in 1792, contains lavender. Originally, it was used to fight migraines.

GIVERNY GARDEN AND

Monet's Water Lilies

When Claude Monet moved to Giverny in 1883, his pink-walled house, dubbed Clos Normand, opened onto an apple orchard. A large boulevard lined with cypress and spruce trees led from the gate to the entrance porch. Monet immediately set to work and never ceased to perfect the Clos Normand to make it the garden of his colorful dreams. He had the box trees uprooted and the spruces cut down, to the great despair of his wife, Alice. Cherry and apricot trees from Japan replaced the apple trees, and flowers covered the ground by the thousands: daffodils, tulips, narcissus, irises, oriental poppies, nasturtiums, roses, and peonies.

THE WATER GARDEN

In 1893, the painter-gardener acquired a swampy piece of land at the end of his garden, located on the other side of the railway line. He diverted the Ru, a small arm of the River Epte, with the intention of turning it into a water garden. A Japanese bridge inspired by one of his prints was built and painted green to stand out from the red traditionally used in Japan. Bamboo, ginkgo biloba, maples, Japanese peonies, lilies, and weeping willows lined the pond.

The flower lover also installed white water lilies, which became his favorite subject in 1905. By trying to re-create the atmosphere of the surface of the sky on which colored spots float, Monet started on a titanic work. In nearly 300 paintings, including some forty large-format ones, this water landscape dotted with water lilies, willow branches, tree reflections, and clouds gave "the illusion of an endless whole, a wave without horizon and shoreline," in the artist's own words.

WATER LILIES AT THE ORANGERY

To celebrate the Allied victory in the First World War, Claude Monet offered *The Water Lilies* to Georges Clemenceau as a gift to France. The year after Monet's death, the Orangerie Museum, located on Place de la Concorde in Paris, hosted the water lily cycle within its walls. Monet's paintings are a true "Sistine of Impressionism," according to the surrealist André Masson in 1952.

ROSE WATER

INGREDIENTS

- Rosewater is used in many drinks. The rule is to add 1 to 1.3 ounces of floral water to 33 ounces of still or sparkling water, or 1.3 to 1.7 ounces to 33 ounces of fruit juice. Decorate with rose petals for a flowery effect.

WATERMELON JUICE AND ROSE WATER

Mix half a peeled and seeded watermelon in a blender. Filter to keep only the juice. Add 2 tablespoons of rose water. Refrigerate and let stand for one hour. Serve well chilled.

LITCHI JUICE AND ROSE WATER

Dilute 8 ounces of litchi juice in 8 ounces of water and add 2 tablespoons of rose water. Decorate with rose petals and raspberry ice cubes.

Rose water comes from the distillation of rose petals and has a very concentrated fragrance. Considered a beauty elixir, it's also used in many recipes.

ORIGAMI ROSES FOR DECORATING YOUR TABLE

MATERIALS

- A square of cardboard
- A pencil
- A pair of scissors
- White glue
- Branches of wood
- A vase

HOW TO

With your pencil, draw a 4-inch spiral on a square sheet of paper. Cut out the spiral. Starting from the outside, wrap the spiral so that it's tight.

A little glue at the base will affix the end of the spiral to the rose. For a nice table decoration, attach the flower to a branch of wood and put it in a vase.

Use the different sheets of paper in this book to make your multicolored roses bloom.

THE SUNFLOWER, A GREAT SUN

What is it?

The sunflower's scientific name, ***Helianthus***, comes from the Greek ***helios*** (sun) and ***anthos*** (flower). It originates in North and South America. In Mexico, the plant has been cultivated for nearly 4,000 years. For the Aztecs, it represented the god of the sun, which is why the flower adorned many temples. As its name suggests—from the Italian ***tornasole***, which rotates with the sun—the sunflower follows the path of the sun. This phenomenon is called heliotropism. In addition to being a lovely flower, its seeds can be eaten roasted and salted, and cooking oil can be extracted from them.

What is its symbolism?

The sunflower symbolizes the sun and love. In Greek mythology, the nymph Clytia fell madly in love with Apollo. But the sun god didn't respond to her advances. Mad with grief, she turned into a sunflower so that her face was always turned toward his chariot.

How does it fit in a bouquet?

It's the essential flower for creating a country bouquet. Gerberas, daisies, or roses form a perfect harmony with the sunflower. With its large yellow flowers, irises, gladioli in blue and purple shades will show it off to its best advantage.

How do you maintain it?

Cut the stems at an angle and crush them with a hammer. Since moisture tends to escape from the leaves, it's best to remove them. Once you've put the sunflower in a vase away from any heat source, regularly replenish the water level, since the sunflower consumes a lot of water.

LEAVES

They are pointed at the tip and a little rough because of their stiff hairs.

FLOWERS

The sunflower has yellow ligulae flowers on the outside and small brownish tubular flowers in the center where the seeds ripen.

COLORS

In addition to its well-known yellow color, the sunflower can also be orange, brown, or dark red.

THE STEM

It can reach a height of thirteen or even thirty feet! When the sunflower is growing, its stem follows the course of the sun to ensure optimal photosynthesis.

SEEDS

The sunflower seed is actually an achene, a dried fruit that is used for its oil.

PERFUME OF POETRY

PERFUME

Reader, have you ever breathed
With drunkenness and slow gluttony
That grain of incense that fills a church,
Or a sachet of inveterate musk?

Deep, magical charm, which grays us
In the present the past restored!
Thus the lover on a beloved body
From memory pluck the exquisite flower.

From her heavy, elastic hair,
Living sachet, alcove censer,
A scent was rising, wild and tawny,

And clothes, muslin or velvet,
All imbued with her pure youth,
There was a fur scent.

Charles Baudelaire

In 1857, Charles Baudelaire published his first collection of poems, *Les Fleurs du mal* (*Flowers of Evil*). The title of the book suggests the idea that one can make something beautiful out of something evil through poetic alchemy. These "sickly flowers," as Baudelaire calls them, were dedicated to the leader of Romanticism, Théophile Gautier.

When it came out, the work caused a scandal. Critics accused it of dealing with macabre subjects. "The odious rubs shoulders with the ignoble. Never before has there been such a review of demons, fetuses, devils, chlorosis, cats and vermin," wrote a critic for *Le Figaro*. Two months later, the book was condemned for "insulting public morals and good morals." Baudelaire was obliged to withdraw six poems.

CHARLES BAUDELAIRE

Les FLEURS du MAL

RELAXING FLOWERS

Flower Bath

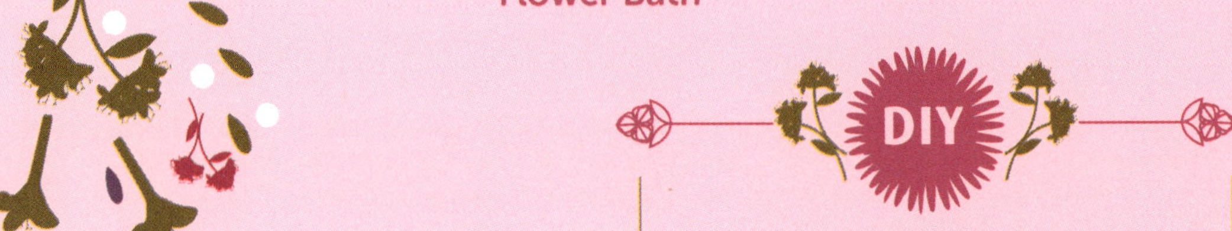

There's nothing more pleasant and soothing than relaxing in a flower-scented bath. Practiced for several millennia, this ritual had already been seducing Cleopatra to preserve the radiance of her skin. The Queen of Egypt used to immerse herself in a bath of donkey's milk and rose petals! It's also said that Marie-Antoinette enjoyed baths with a thousand flowers.

There's nothing better to make you feel good than a sachet of dried flowers for your bath. Rose and lavender, chamomile, rosemary, and basil, or a tangy mixture of lemon balm and lemon peel—all these flowers and citrus fruits can make up a scented sachet for the bath.

A BAG OF DRIED FLOWERS FOR THE BATH

MATERIALS

- A square of muslin
- Dried calendula and chamomile and lavender flowers, rose petals
- Oat flour
- String or piece of wool

HOW TO

In a square of muslin or gauze, or in the end of a nylon stocking, place 2 tablespoons of dried calendula flowers along with chamomile flowers, lavender flowers, and rose petals. Sprinkle the mixture with oatmeal and add a few drops of essential oil. Using a string or a piece of wool, close the bag without squeezing too tightly, to avoid crushing the flowers. Attach it to the bathtub faucet and turn the water on. Once your bath is ready, let the bag infuse. Farewell fatigue and stress; relax in the bath and gently rub your body with this soothing bath bag, which is as good for the skin as for the mind.

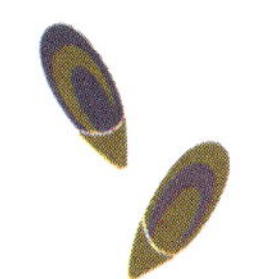

LAVENDER

This purplish-blue plant owes its name to the Latin *lavare* (to wash). In ancient Rome, its flowers were used for bathing or to perfume washed clothes. Its scent is known for its soothing properties. It promotes sleep, reduces anxiety, and even has analgesic properties. Pour 1 or 2 ounces of dried flowers in 33 ounces of boiling water. Leave to infuse for about fifteen minutes, then add this mixture to the bath water just before getting into it.

VALERIAN

With its clusters of purple, white, or pinkish flowers, valerian is best known for its roots, which secrete an anxiolytic substance. In the time of Hippocrates, it was used crushed in sachets placed under the pillow to soothe anxieties, but also to ward off evil spirits. Particularly appreciated by cats—hence its nickname "catnip"—it was also believed to have aphrodisiac powers!

MARJORAM

This plant, whose flavor is very appreciated in cooking, helps relieve anxiety, nervous tension, and insomnia. The essential oil, extracted from the leaves and flowers, has a woody, herbaceous, and fresh scent. It's also a powerful antibacterial for the respiratory tract. Its dried leaves can be used to fill relaxing cushions.

HANAMI

The Cherry Blossom Festival

In Japanese, *hanami*—literally translated "flower" and "see"—refers to a tradition that dates back to the eighth century: the contemplation of cherry flowers. During the time of Nara, the plum blossom freshly imported from China was fashionable.

Later on, flowering cherry or sakura replaced it. The flowering of the cherry trees (*Prunus*) coincided with the beginning of the rice-planting season and with the resumption of other agricultural activities. Offerings to the gods were deposited at the foot of the trees, and the peasants drank sake in the gods' honor. Japanese cherry trees also symbolize the ephemeral nature of existence. A century later, the imperial court celebrated the first hanami at the Shinsen-en garden in Kyoto, and it was declared a holiday among the gentry. The custom was taken up by the samurai, then by the people, and finally became a national tradition.

JAPANESE RITUAL

Contemplating cherry trees in bloom (*unemi*) is a ritual in the Land of the Rising Sun. Every town has its own places to stroll in the shade of these delicate pink-tinted flowers. In parks and gardens, the inhabitants spread large tablecloths under the cherry blossoms and settle down to picnic with family and friends. The sakuramochi, a rice cake wrapped in a cherry leaf, is in every store window. It's also an opportunity to sing and dance. During the Miyako Odori festival held in Kyoto every spring, the *maiko*, apprentice geisha, celebrate this ephemeral flowering by performing the cherry tree dance.

Spring night comes to an end, the day dawns on the cherry trees

Matsuo Basho

CANDIED-VIOLET RECIPE

INGREDIENTS

- Violets
- 1 egg white
- 1 bowl granulated sugar

Beat the egg white with a fork and dunk the flowers completely into it.

Place each flower on a sheet of baking paper, sprinkle them with sugar, and leave them to air-dry for four to five days. Once dry, the flowers should be stiff.

You can use all sorts of edible flowers: pansy, nigella, rose, cornflower, and nasturtium.

Use the gift tags to offer your candied violets in a violet-patterned box.

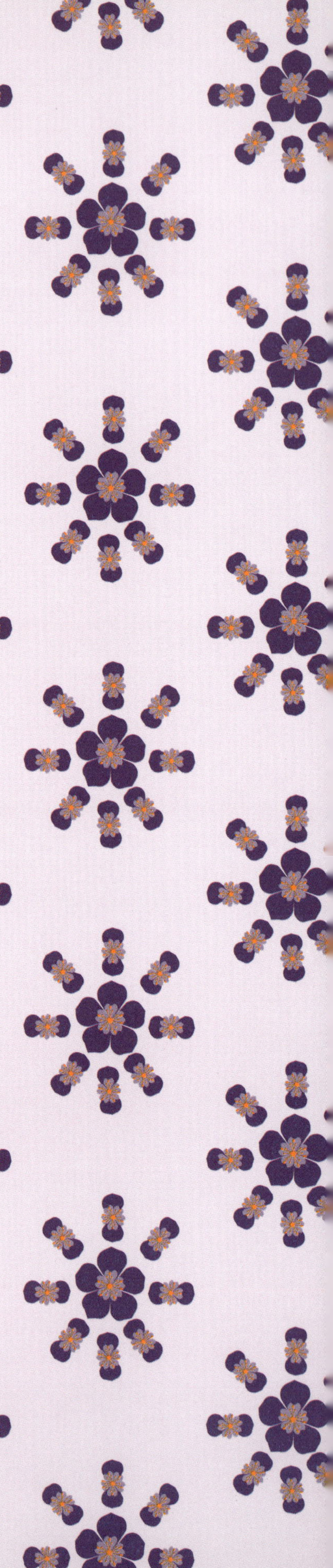

FLOWER LOLLIPOPS RECIPE

INGREDIENTS

- 7 oz. sugar
- 3 tablespoons flavored syrup
- 1 tablespoon water
- A few drops food coloring
- 1 teaspoon lemon juice
- Lollipop sticks and baking paper
- A lollipop mold
- Flower petals: pansy, nigella, rose, cornflower, lavender, nasturtium, violet, or jasmine

Pour the sugar, syrup, water, and lemon juice into a saucepan. Heat to boiling, or ideally to 300°F, and then add the food coloring.

Spoon the mixture onto baking paper or into a lollipop mold. Add the petals and the sticks in the center. Turn out of the mold after one hour.

Wrap and label your flower lollipops.

THE PEONY, HEALING FLOWER

What is it?

Today, peonies are appreciated for the beauty of their flowers and their incredible fragrance. Nevertheless, this plant, which takes its name from the Greek *Paeonia*—literally "fit to heal"—was highly appreciated for its healing virtues thousands of years ago. Long before it adorned imperial palaces and inspired artists, it was used by the Chinese, who considered it the queen of flowers, as a medicinal plant. Japan also became its second homeland. It's still widely cultivated for the production of medicines made from the bark of its roots.

What is its symbolism?

In China, the peony is associated with feminine beauty and love, but it also symbolizes wealth and honor. In the West, the peony is a sign of sincerity and shyness. Hence the expression "blushing like a peony," which comes from the shame felt by the nymph Peony, who was transformed into a peony flower.

How does it fit in a bouquet?

Majestic, the peony is self-sufficient. You are free to mix the colors and add a few cordyline leaves that look like a palm or eucalyptus tree. However, it goes well with other flowers such as lisianthus, rose, lilac, and, of course, its cousin, the ranunculus.

How do you maintain it?

In a vase, peonies last four to seven days. To enjoy them for as long as possible, it's best to pick them as buds. To help them bloom, spray them with water from time to time and regularly remove withered leaves. Peonies are very sensitive to light and heat. Immerse their stems in a large volume of water.

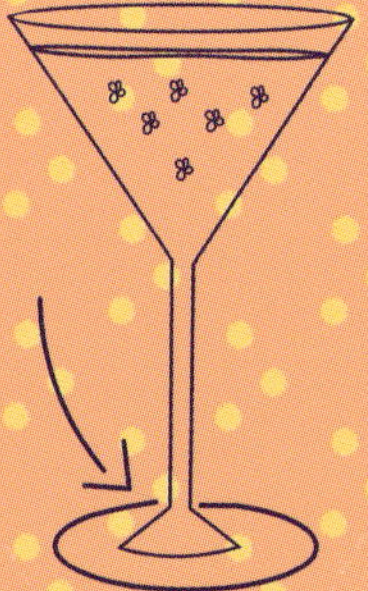

FLOWERS

Thick and nicely ruffled, they can be simple, half-double, double, bulging, or Japanese. A little capricious, the peony can take between two and five years to flower.

LEAVES

A distinction is made between herbaceous peonies, whose stems and leaves die off in winter, and shrubs, with developed woody stems and deciduous foliage.

STEM

In the herbaceous peony, the stem is erect and tinged with red. This plant owes its longevity to its deep roots that protect it from the vagaries of the climate.

COLORS

White, pink, red, or yellow, the peony flower comes in a multitude of shades.

IN THE NAME OF A FLOWER!

These timeless flowery names reveal their history and the character of those who bear them.

MARGUERITE

This small flower with a yellow heart and white petals comes from the Greek word ***margaritês***, which means "pearl." Many crowned heads have borne this name. Marguerite de Bourgogne and Marguerite de Valois became famous for marrying and deceiving two kings of France!

Character traits: hardworking, idealistic, altruistic, honest, compassionate

ANEMONE

The Greeks named this flower such because it opened up at the slightest breath of wind, spreading its pollen over the land. One of the nymphs in mythology is named after it.

Character traits: adventurous, fanciful, funny, passionate, willing

IRIS

Taking her name from the Greek ***iridos***, meaning "rainbow," Iris is a nymph in Greek mythology, messenger of the gods. The Greeks depicted her as a graceful young girl wearing a rainbow as a scarf.

Character traits: self-confident, daring, independent, dynamic, energetic, spontaneous

VIOLET

This delicately scented little flower is the emblem of Toulouse. It's said that the nymph Io, courted by Apollo, refused him. Outraged, the god transformed her into a chaste and modest flower, the violet. Since then, the flower has been associated with modesty and shyness.

Character traits: human, emotional, generous, dreamy, reserved

GARANCE

This plant with yellow flowers and red roots thrives in warm regions. It was once used to dye fabrics bright red. Garance is celebrated on October 5, the day of Saint Fleur, a fourteenth-century nun who lived among the sick and looked after them.

Character traits: structured, persevering, sympathetic

EGLANTINE

This name comes from the Latin ***aculeatus***, meaning "thorny." The rosehip plant, a wild rose, can live up to a thousand years. Its pale-pink petals are heart shaped.

Character traits: charming, cheerful, sensitive, gentle, determined, benevolent

LILA

This name has a slightly different spelling than the plant from which it comes—the lilac shrub with highly fragrant white or purple flowers. In Hebrew, lilac means "what belongs to me is hers."

Character traits: joyful, philosopher, strategist, leader, spiritual.

CAPUCHIN

Native to South America, this flower, which was called "Peruvian watercress" in the eighteenth century, produces flowers with bright and exuberant colors. Edible, it has a slightly sweet taste. In gardens, it attracts aphids and thus preserves its neighbors.

Character traits: dreamy, human, sensitive

APHRODISIAC

Carnal Flowers

Throughout history, flowers have often been considered to have an influence on romantic relationships. Cupid's dart with its blue petals is a good example. It owes its name to its aphrodisiac properties and was once used in love potions.

Saffron is also said to be a love stimulant. Cleopatra used it in her bath to spice up her sex life. The Egyptians prepared a love potion with savory; hence its nickname, "love herb." It was also said to have beneficial effects on women's fertility.

And the orchid wasn't given its name by chance, since the Greek word *orchis*, for the plant's bulb, means "testicle." Until recently, orchid bulbs were harvested and worn as amulets or powdered and then made into love potions.

MAKE A VANILLA MASSAGE OIL

INGREDIENTS

- 3 sticks of vanilla
- 12 fluid oz. jojoba oil

HOW TO

Split the vanilla sticks lengthwise with the tip of a knife and scrape out the seeds. Cut the hollowed-out sticks into pieces. Pour the jojoba oil into a bottle and then add the seeds and vanilla sticks. Place the mixture in a dark place for two months, shaking the bottle daily. Jojoba oil has the best and longest shelf life of all the vegetable oils. You can keep it for at least a year.

VANILLA

Vanilla is the fruit of an orchid (the ***Vanilla planifolia)*** that grows in the undergrowth of warm and humid tropical forests, . In Latin America, vanilla sticks are used to make love potions, because beyond their sweet, rich, and familiar scent, they have aphrodisiac virtues. It's also the flower of relaxing and sensual massages par excellence.

YLANG-YLANG

This tree can grow up to 30 feet high and has beautiful, yellow, star-shaped flowers. The scent of ylang-ylang, meaning "flower of flowers" in Filipino, rivals that of jasmine and rose. In the Indian Ocean islands where it's grown, it's considered an aphrodisiac. In Indonesia, the tradition is to cover the bridal bed with these flowers.

JASMINE

Highly appreciated in perfumery, jasmine appears in many romantic tales. For example, Cleopatra is said to have met Mark Antony while sailing on a boat whose sails were soaked in jasmine essence to seduce him. In India, there is a legend that the god of carnal love reached his victims with arrows decorated with a sprig of jasmine. Since then, no Hindu wedding has been celebrated without this flower; it symbolizes eternal love between the newlyweds.

LILY OF THE VALLEY

May 1

The tradition of offering lily of the valley dates back to Charles IX. On May 1, 1561, the young king and his mother, Catherine de Medici, visited Louis de Girard de Maisonforte in his garden. During their walk, the knight offered the king a sprig of lily of the valley as a good-luck charm. Charmed by this delicate attention, Charles decided to do the same with the ladies of the court the following year, and it became an annual tradition.

WORK SYMBOL

Initially a lucky flower, the lily of the valley also became the symbol of work. One hundred years after the French Revolution, on the first International Workers' Day launched by the international Socialists, the demonstrators wore a red triangle in their button-holes, quickly replaced by a dog rose. This Socialist flower paid homage to Fabre d'Eglantine, the creator of the revolutionary calendar. Beginning in 1907, a few sprigs of lily of the valley tied with a red ribbon began to appear. The bell flower flourished in parades, so much so that the press spoke of the marriage of the lily of the valley and the dog rose. In 1941, Marshal Pétain instituted Labor and Social Agreement Day on May 1. The red rose then definitively gave way to lily of the valley.

FASHIONABLE FLOWER

Lily of the valley is a favorite of artists and designers. Félix Mayol, the early-twentieth-century songwriter from Toulon, used to hang a sprig of lily of the valley on the back of his frock coat. The bells then became the emblem of happiness for his fans. Christian Dior cherished this spring flower so much that his regular florist grew it all year round in a specially heated greenhouse! So, summer and winter alike, he could wear one in his buttonhole. He also kept some at the bottom of his pocket, in a small ornate box, as a good luck charm. And every May 1, all his workers and clients were offered a sprig of lily of the valley. But his dream was to capture the aroma of this delicate flower. Thanks to the talents of his master perfumer, Diorissimo perfume was born.

FLORAL SPICE

SAFFRON

Native to the East, saffron is the dried pistil of purple flowers of a variety of crocus, the *Crocus sativus*. It takes about 150 flowers to obtain half an ounce of saffron, which explains its high price. The flowers have to be picked by hand very early in the morning.

IN COOKING

Saffron is used to balance the taste of salty and sweet dishes. Yellow-orange in color, it has a particular smell—a little pungent and very fine. It's used in almost all the cuisines of the world. It's found in the Moroccan tagine, Indian biryani and curry, Milanese risotto, Valencia paella, and Marseilles bouillabaisse. It's also used in desserts to flavor roasted fruit, biscuits, roasted fruit, cookies, or cakes.

To incorporate saffron into preparations, the secret is to infuse the pistils in hot water or cream for two to twelve hours. It should be added halfway through cooking, since it takes some time for its aromas to disperse, while prolonged cooking dissipates them.

FLORAL SPICE

CLOVE

The clove is the flower bud of the clove tree, a large tree native to the Moluccas archipelago in Indonesia. Before the flower blooms, the folded petals form a small ball in the center of the bud. This is the head. Red when picked, it turns brown when dry.

IN COOKING

The aroma of cloves is penetrating, warm, and rich. Its taste is both pungent and bitter. It's part of most spice blends: Indian garam masala, Ethiopian curry, and five-spice blend. When ground, it's used for meats, Indian curries, Ethiopian curries, marinades, sauces, and pickles in French, Asian, African, and Middle Eastern cooking. It flavors gingerbread and mulled wine, which are very popular at Christmas. Stuck in an onion, the heads of cloves are a must in stews or cabbage soup.

Cloves can be kept for several years in an airtight bottle, away from heat and light. When ground, they lose their aromatic intensity more quickly.

WHO'S WHO

FREESIA, DELICIOUSLY FRAGRANT

What is it?

Belonging to the Iridaceae family, the freesia was discovered in South Africa. It was named in the mid-nineteenth century by the Danish botanist Christian Friedrich Ecklon in homage to one of his students, the German botanist and physician Friedrich Heinrich Theodor Freese. It's also known as Cape lily of the valley because of its flowers, which grow in clusters. Freesia comes in sparkling colors and has a delicate, subtle fragrance that makes it one of the most widely used flowers in perfumery. Its fruity notes, similar to those of orange blossom, are present in famous perfumes such as Armani's Acqua Di Giò for Men.

What is its symbolism?

The freesia symbolizes unconditional love . . . love and innocence, but also resistance. Therefore, you can offer white freesias after seven years of marriage. It's also the flower of youth.

How does it fit in a bouquet?

Beneath its delicate appearance lies a rather robust flower that is particularly majestic when alone. Wheatears or anthurium leaves, ferns or aralias leaves will elevate this bouquet. Freesias can be combined with almost all flowers: tulips, irises, sea lavender, roses, and more.

How do you maintain it?

The buttons at the top of the stem rarely open. To stimulate flowering of the lower ones, remove wilted flowers from the base of the stems by pinching them with your fingers. Like all bulb flowers, freesias need very little water: fill the vase only two-thirds full.

FLOWERS

Giving off a subtle perfume, they develop in clusters and are arranged laterally at the end of a curved stem.

STEM

Thin but sturdy, it's connected to the bulb, which forms small tubers called "pearls" under the ground.

LEAVES

Elongated and flat, they are reminiscent of its cousins in the Iridaceae family—gladioli and irises.

COLORS

Red, orange, yellow, blue, purple, white, or pink, the freesia exists in a wide variety of bright colors; some varieties are bicolor and multicolored.

MAKE ME A FLOWER!

Flowers offer a beautiful bouquet of sentimental expressions!

BLUE FLOWER

In the language of flowers, blue evokes mystery, delicacy, pure feelings, tender love, and shyness. We owe this expression to the German romantic writer Novalis's unfinished novel at the beginning of the nineteenth century. A blue flower is presented as the passage between the real and chaotic world and the spiritual world in which the artist takes refuge to flee reality and to grow spiritually. It also symbolizes absolute love that the young hero carries to Mathilde.

ARTICHOKE'S HEART

The artichoke is the bud of a plant that is eaten before it blooms into a beautiful purple flower. Like the daisy, from which the petals are removed one by one to know the intensity of one's love, the artichoke is eaten leaf after leaf to reach the heart, the quintessence of this leafy vegetable. It represents someone who gives his love easily. He gives part of his heart to as many people as there are leaves surrounding an artichoke's heart!

WHISPER SWEET NOTHINGS

This expression comes from the gentlemen of the seventeenth century who courted their sweetheart with compliments and gallant words. It was not a question of counting the little flowers they offered to their beloved, but of inventing a story to be told to entertain her. In those days, the terms "flowers" or "little flowers" were used to refer to nonsense.

LET THE CAT OUT OF THE BAG

Several hypotheses can explain this expression dating from the thirteenth century. At that time, women kept the sweet words of their lovers in a small box. Why does this expression refer to the rose? Because at the time, this delicate flower was used to compose rare and precious perfumes.

BLUSH LIKE A PEONY

Red is the color of strong emotions. Thus, when blood rises to the cheeks, it indicates a feeling that one would prefer to keep hidden. Greek mythology tells that the nymph Peony, after breaking the code of modesty, was transformed into a peony. Hence this expression, which suggests shame.

HE LOVES ME, HE LOVES ME NOT

This romantic game consists of removing one by one the petals of a daisy while singing for fun or superstition: "He loves me a little, a lot, madly, passionately, not at all." The last petal that is removed is supposed to reveal the intensity of love. This expression also evokes the sensual art of stripping in cabarets.

FLORASCOPE

Born under the sign of a flower

Just as there is a language of flowers, there is an astrological floral guide. The zodiac sign that's related to your date of birth may not control your destiny, but it can open the door to floral astrology. The floral horoscope is not new. Antique texts mentioned links between the tulip and people born under the sign of Aries. Each zodiac sign corresponds to a specific flower and lucky charm. Indeed, the stars are not the only things that can reveal aspects of your personality. The flowers also have a say and have their own distinctive signature. Looking for a bouquet to offer a loved one? Let yourself be inspired by the stars and discover the totem flowers of each sign of the zodiac. Just like the language of flowers, where each species is a symbol that conveys a hidden message, floral astrology is a way to make the stars speak through flowers.

ARIES
THE TULIP

Impulsive and spontaneous with an intensely passionate side, Aries has the tulip as its favorite flower.

TAURUS
THE ROSE

Underneath his stubborn airs, Taurus is also a great romantic. That's why the rose is a perfect match for him.

GEMINI
POET'S CARNATION

Versatile and expressive, Gemini is charismatic just like the poet's carnation that attracts bees in the summer.

CANCER
THE CAMELLIA

Of a sensitive and protective temperament, Cancer is associated with round and delicate flowers, such as a camellia.

LEO
THE SUNFLOWER

What other flower than the sunflower, the incarnation of the sun, resembles the mane of the king of the jungle?

VIRGO
THE LILY

Symbol of purity and virginity, the lily flower is in perfect harmony with Virgo.

LIBRA
THE GLADIOLI

With its delicately pleated petals in pink hues, the gladiola symbolizes the altruism and gentleness that characterizes Libra.

SCORPIO
THE THISTLE

With its small, prickly leaves, the thistle is like Scorpio: beautiful to look at, but dangerous to touch.

SAGITTARIUS
THE MIMOSA

The small yellow balls of the mimosa perfectly reflect the jovial nature and inexhaustible energy of Sagittarius.

CAPRICORN
THE HYDRANGEA

Capricorns are tender and affectionate. If there is one flower that combines these qualities, it's the hydrangea.

AQUARIUS
THE PEONY

This flower is a sign of sincerity and shyness. Just like Aquarius, known to be reserved and loyal.

PISCES
THE WATER LILY

The water lily grows in water, which explains the link between this plant and the sign of Pisces.

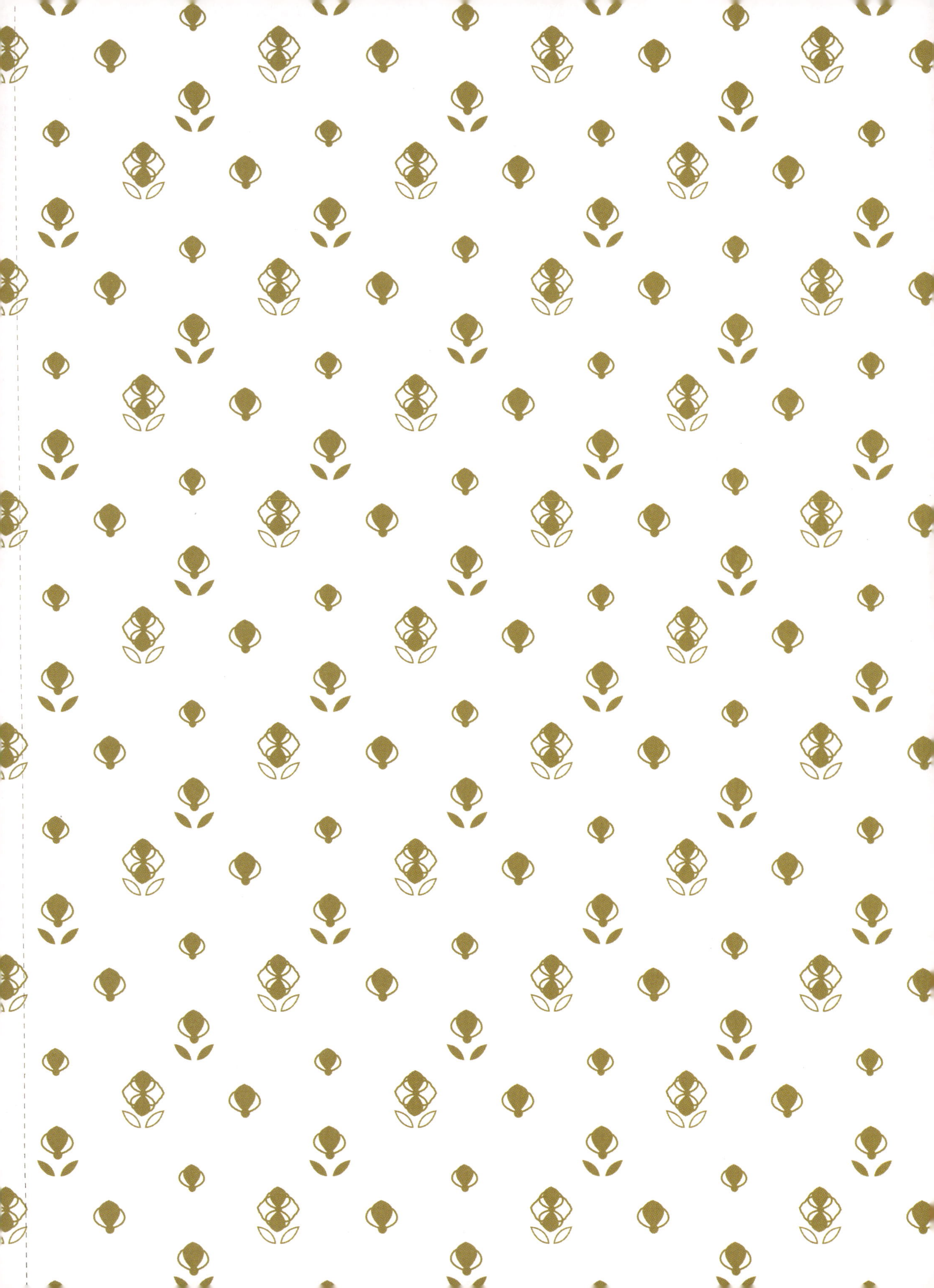

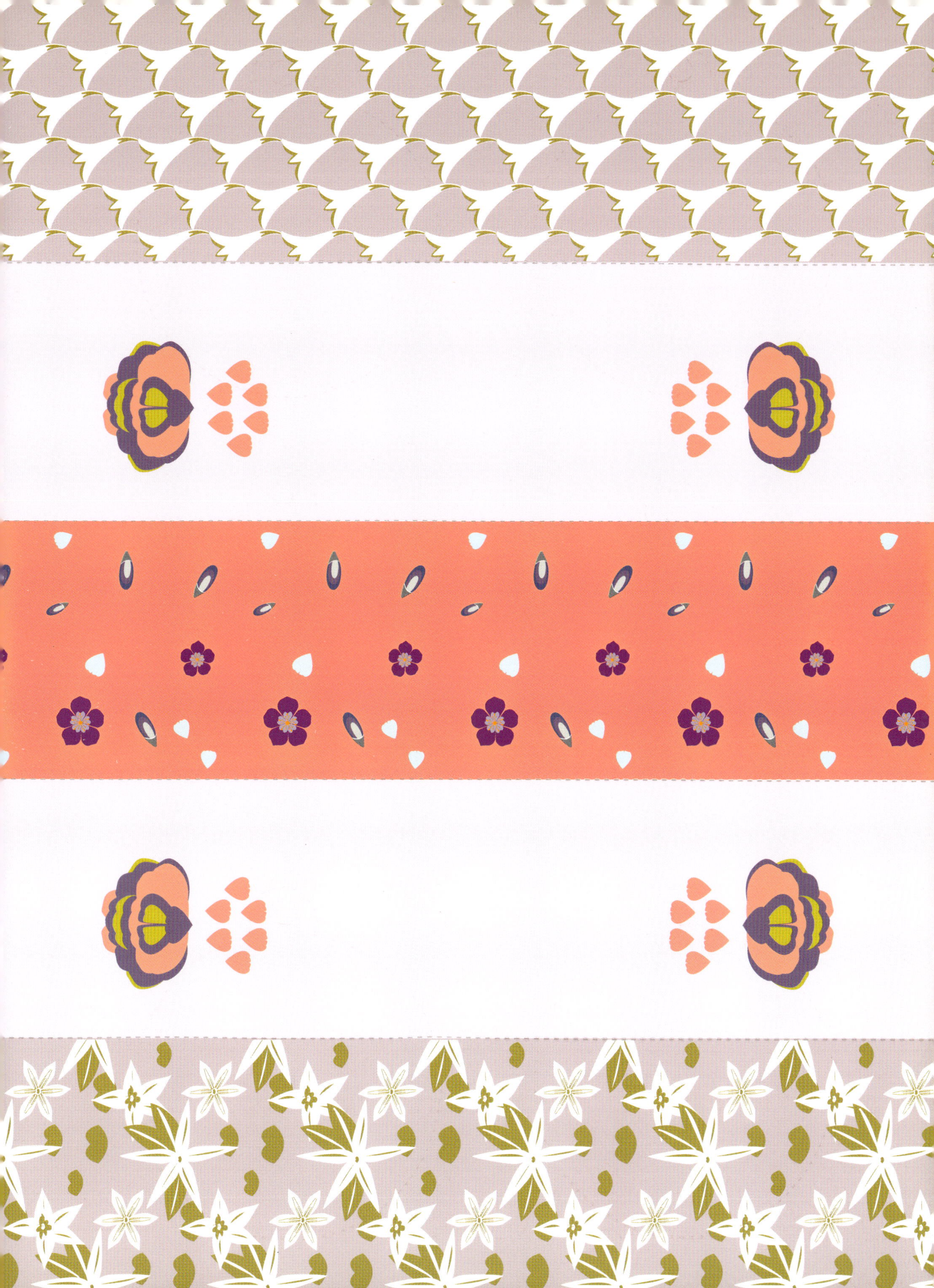

THE MYTH OF
Narcissus

Son of the river god Cephissus and the nymph Liriope, Narcissus was destined for a long life, according to the words of the blind soothsayer Tiresias, with one condition: never contemplate his own image. As he grew up, the young hunter was extremely handsome. Nymphs fell instantly in love with him at first sight, among them, Echo. However, Narcissus was insensitive to feelings that he aroused and rejected his suitors one by one. Madly in love and inconsolable, Echo implored Nemesis, the great goddess of righteous anger, to cast a spell on the one who spurned her.

NARCISSISM

One day, on his way home from hunting, Narcissus was taken by a sudden urge to drink. As he bent down to quench his thirst in a lake, he saw his reflection and immediately fell in love with it. Yet, he was unable to reach this beauty, for every time he tried to kiss it, his face would flee, but he could not move away from it either: "I am burning with love for myself, and yet, how can I approach this beauty that I see reflected in the water? But I cannot move away from it. Only death will deliver me," relates the poet Ovid in *The Metamorphoses*. The story tells that at the place where he perished, a white flower grew. This plant likes damp places and was named narcissus in memory of the young man's obsession with his reflection in the water.

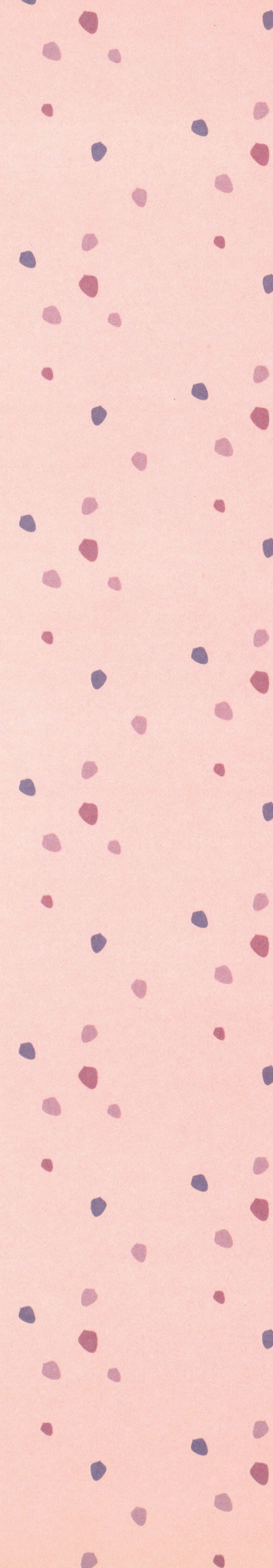

RECIPE

FRUIT SALAD WITH WISTERIA FLOWERS

INGREDIENTS

- 1 bunch of wisteria
- 1 celery stalk
- 1 apple
- 1 sprig of tarragon
- 1 lemon
- Olive oil

Wash the wisteria and remove each flower from the stems. Put to one side.

Wash the celery, apple, and tarragon. Thinly slice the celery. Dice the apple. Chop the tarragon. Mix the ingredients in a bowl and simply sprinkle with lemon and olive oil. Serve immediately.

RECIPE

CITRUS AND BEGONIA SALAD

INGREDIENTS

- 20 begonia flowers
- 1 grapefruit
- 1 orange
- 1 clementine
- 1 cooked beetroot
- 2 scoops of buffalo mozzarella
- 1 handful of coriander seeds
- Some mint leaves
- Olive oil
- Salt, pepper

Peel the citrus fruits and slice the beetroot and mozzarella.

Arrange the grapefruit, orange, clementine, beetroot, and mozzarella on each plate. Add the begonia flowers, chopped mint, and a drizzle of olive oil. Crush the coriander seeds between two spoons to release their flavor. Season with salt and pepper. Serve immediately.

Begonia flowers have a tangy, crunchy taste and a juicy flavor.

WHO'S WHO

THE MIMOSA, A WINTER SUN

What is it?

Imported from Australia by British botanists at the beginning of the nineteenth century, the mimosa illuminates the gardens of the French Riviera with its small, fragrant, and fluffy golden balls. The town of Mandelieu-la-Napoule, in the Alpes-Maritimes, is the international mimosa capital, where, since 1931, a popular annual festival has been held in February. The tree has even given its name to a town in the Var: Bormes-les-Mimosas. Now 80 miles long, the mimosa road links Bormes-les-Mimosas to Grasse, where the mimosa is exploited for its essences and has contributed, like the rose, to the development of the cosmetics industry. In the Alpes-Maritimes and the Var, nearly eighteen million mimosa stems are produced every year. The best-known species is commonly known as the florist's mimosa or *Acacia dealbata*.

What is its symbolism?

With its lemon-yellow pom-poms, the mimosa is luminous. This winter flower exudes optimism, cheerfulness, and tenderness and delivers a message of friendship. It also symbolizes feminine energy. In Italy, it's the emblem of Women's Day, March 8.

How does it fit in a bouquet?

If the mimosa is self-sufficient, it also adapts to all associations: tulip, anemone, rose, lily, pansy. Its fragrant and fluffy yellow flowers are perfect with the blue of the iris or hyacinth.

How do you maintain it?

The mimosa does not like temperatures above 60°F. Place the bouquet outside or in the coolest room of the house. To speed up flowering, soak the stems for five minutes in boiling salted water, then immerse them in a vase of cold water.

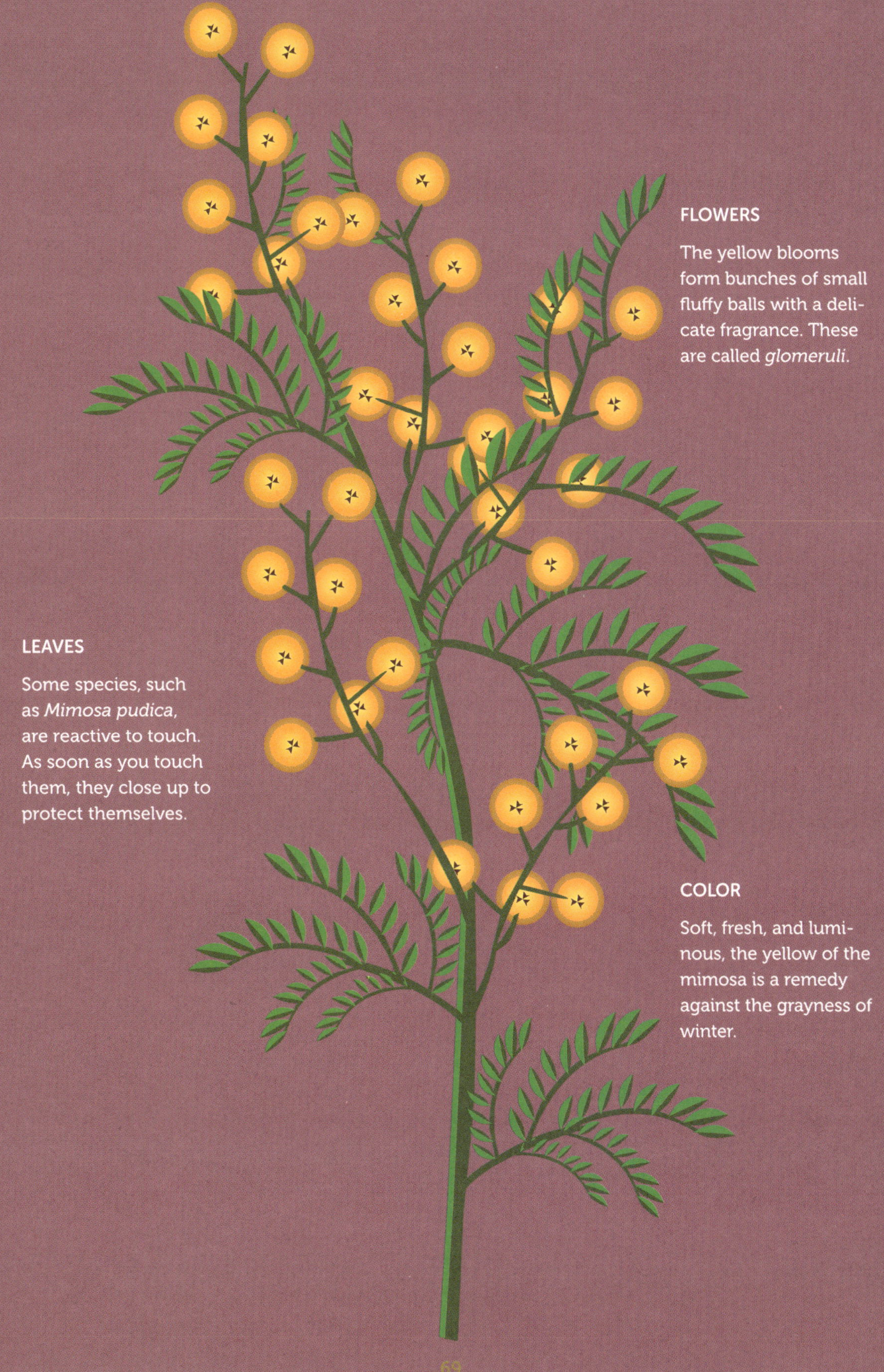

FLOWERS

The yellow blooms form bunches of small fluffy balls with a delicate fragrance. These are called *glomeruli*.

LEAVES

Some species, such as *Mimosa pudica*, are reactive to touch. As soon as you touch them, they close up to protect themselves.

COLOR

Soft, fresh, and luminous, the yellow of the mimosa is a remedy against the grayness of winter.

THESE GREAT HEROINES

From Alexandre Dumas to Honoré de Balzac, many writers have been inspired to give life to heroines with the sweet names of flowers.

THE LADY OF THE CAMELLIAS

Alexandre Dumas

A famous courtesan during the reign of Louis-Philippe, Marie Duplessis was the great love of Alexandre Dumas's son, who was inspired by their story to write this novel, published in 1848. The young woman, suffering from tuberculosis, wore a beautiful camellia on her shoulder when she went to the theater. At that time, the camellia was a fashionable flower, mainly cultivated for decorating blouses and buttonholes. An invoice from its florist located on the rue de la Paix in Paris testifies to the young woman's passion for the camellia: she wore a white camellia for twenty-five days of the month, and on the other five days, a red camellia.

THE LILY OF THE VALLEY

Honoré de Balzac

In this sentimental novel, among the best-known works of Honoré de Balzac, the hero, Felix de Vandenesse, addresses a letter to his fiancée, Natalie de Manerville, in which he tells her about his first passion for the Countess Henriette de Mortsauf. A married woman, mother of two fragile children, she embodies the purity and the nobility of virtue as the lilies of the Indre valley. The book was published in the same year as the death of Laure de Berny, Balzac's great love.

MADAME CHRYSANTHEMUM

Pierre Loti

Flowers punctuated the life of the young French army admiral Pierre Viaud. During an expedition to Polynesia, the Queen of Tahiti Pomaré, with whom he had a love affair, gave him the name of a flower that would become his pen name, Loti (a rose, a priori). A few years later, during a trip to Nagasaki, he married a young Japanese woman for a month and left her. This story inspired him to write *Madame Chrysanthemum*. This famous romance novel in turn inspired Puccini's famous opera *Madame Butterfly*.

MAKE A JAPANESE PAPER BOOKMARK

MATERIALS

- Use the flowery Japanese paper in this book to make your bookmark.
- A 7.5-by-10-inch sheet of card paper
- 4 inches of ribbon
- White glue
- A flat brush
- A hole punch

HOW TO

Cut a rectangle 2 to 3 inches wide out of the card paper. With the brush, paint a thin layer of glue onto the card. Gently apply it to the reverse side of the Japanese paper, chasing out any air bubbles. Place on a table and put one or more books on it while it's drying. Make a hole at the top in the center of the bookmark with the punch. Fold the ribbon in half and tie a knot: pass the loop of ribbon through the hole, then slip the ends of the ribbon into this loop and tighten gently. Your bookmark is ready to be used or offered!

MAGIC

The Mysterious Mandrake

The mandrake is a plant surrounded by mysteries. Since the Middle Ages, it has been said to have magical powers—to make one invisible, to ward off bad luck at cards, to predict the future. It's also said to bring wealth and make women fertile. Associated with toxic plants such as datura, henbane, or belladonna, mandrake was used in the composition of ointments and evil magic potions. It has the rather banal appearance of a low plant with broad leaves, with berries that look like small apples. However, its root is exuberant and strangely resembles genitalia, feminine as well as masculine.

A story was told that the most beautiful mandrake specimens grew at the foot of gallows. Another legend said that the plant screamed when uprooted. This is why a dog was given the task—a rope was tied to the root, and the end was tied around the dog's neck. The plant was uprooted when the dog was chased off. Reputedly, the animal did not survive. These rumors made it possible for quacks to sell the plant at a high price, so much so that in 1690, the price of a specimen could be as high as a craftsman's annual salary.

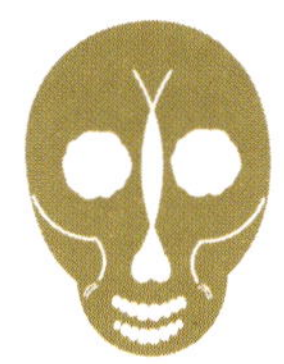

DATURA

Datura is nicknamed "devil's grass" or "grass of the devil." This very toxic plant is native to India. It's associated with Shiva, the god of creation, but also of the destruction of nature. He was in charge of making the bewitched lose his memory after having made him commit the blackest actions. The plant also has aphrodisiac virtues. Peruvians prepared a sexy drink by macerating its flowers in corn beer.

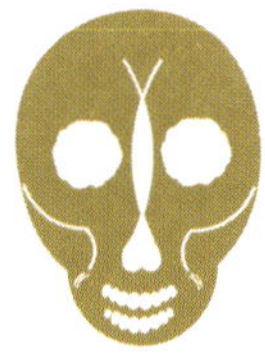

BELLADONNA

Belladonna was also used in magic ointments. Those who tasted it felt as if they were flying and moving at the speed of the wind. It has been proven that belladonna causes the acceleration and amplification of perceptions.

POPPY

Along with henbane and mandrake, the poppy, from which opium is extracted, is the basis of the famous theriac. This pharmaceutical preparation created by Hippocrates appeared until 1884 in the French pharmacopoeia, even if the prolonged use of this substance kills as surely as the cruelest of witches.

The Ukrainian Flower Wreath

In Ukraine, flowers are sacred and considered as gifts from God. The wreath of flowers, called a *vinok*, is inseparable from the traditional costume. Young girls originally wore this headdress in spring as a sign of their purity and to ward off evil spirits. Like a talisman, it was also hung in a tree or in an attic to protect the house from lightning.

A PROTECTIVE CHARM

An old legend tells the story of a young girl wearing the vinok who, while walking in a forest, met a handsome young man. He promised to marry her if she took it off. Unable to resist the charm of the handsome stranger, she took off her crown, and the young man turned into a devil and kidnapped her. Since that day, the crown of flowers has been seen as a protective charm.

SYMBOLIC FLOWERS

The Ukrainian vinok can contain up to twelve different varieties of flowers, each with its own meaning. The yarrow symbolizes insubordination; cherry blossoms, maternal love; the viburnum, feminine beauty; the daisy, tenderness; the cornflower and chamomile, health. The color of the ribbon that you weave with the braid also has a meaning: green evokes spring, blue evokes the sky, white is purity, and red is love. The festival of Ivan Kupala, celebrated at the beginning of July, is when Ukrainian women make a bonnet of flowers they put in the river. The waters then carry it to their future husband.

BRAID A GARLAND OF FLOWERS

MATERIALS

- Fresh flowers (roses, gypsophila, delphinium, thistle flowers)
- Wire
- Sheers
- String or ribbon
- Floral adhesive

HOW TO

Cut the wire to the size of the circumference of your head. Make a loop on each side of the wire and slide the string through it to fit your head perfectly. Tie a knot and fix it with floral adhesive. Intertwine the wire with resistant foliage (ivy), then assemble a few flowers to form small bouquets. Insert them into the wire and fix them with floral adhesive.

RECIPE

LEMON AND LAVENDER CAKE

INGREDIENTS

- 1 cup soft butter
- ⅓ cup brown sugar
- 1 pinch of salt
- ⅔ cup mountain honey
- 3 eggs
- 1½ cups self-rising flour
- The juice of 1 lemon
- Untreated, dried real lavender flowers

Preheat the oven to 350°F. Heat the lemon juice with 2 teaspoons of dried lavender and leave to infuse.

Cream the butter with the sugar to obtain a homogeneous mixture. Add salt and honey, mix, then add the eggs one by one.

Filter the lemon juice with lavender and add it to the mixture. Finish with the sifted flour and mix.

Fill a cake tin with the dough and bake for forty-five minutes.

Lavender has a strong taste, so use it sparingly.

RECIPE

MIRABELLE PLUM AND MEADOWSWEET SORBET

INGREDIENTS

- 2 pounds mirabelle plums
- ½ pound meadowsweet petals
- The juice of 1 lemon
- 4 gallons of water
- ½ cup sugar

Wash and stone the mirabelle plums. Cook them in a saucepan for fifteen minutes with the sugar.

Infuse the meadowsweet for fifteen minutes in simmering water. Filter.

In a mixing bowl, pour the compote, the infused water, and the lemon juice. Mix and let cool. If necessary, add the sugar, then put to freeze in an ice-cream maker.

Slightly aniseed and sweet, meadowsweet is reminiscent of bitter almond, with a hint of vanilla. It's nicknamed the "poor man's vanilla."

THE CARNATION, DIVINE FLOWER

What is it?

Native to the Mediterranean basin, the carnation has been known for more than 2,000 years. The Romans used it to make garlands for athletes and to make toilette water. Its botanical name is *Dianthus*, a name derived from the Greek words *dios* (god) and *anthos* (flower). It's therefore a divine flower! In the Catholic religion, it's associated with the Virgin Mary. When Jesus was crucified, Mary shed tears that became pink carnations. In Leonardo da Vinci's painting, she is depicted holding the flower in her hand. The pink carnation thus represents the unconditional love of a mother. In France, this ornamental plant was commercialized from the fifteenth century onward.

What is its symbolism?

Like the rose, the meaning of the carnation depends on its color: white for pure love, bright red for deep love. Renaissance painters liked to place this flower in love scenes. During the course of history, the carnation also expressed political commitment: it became the symbol of the movement of the Bonapartists, Jacobins, and Portuguese militants during the Carnation Revolution.

How does it fit in a bouquet?

With its beautiful, fragrant flowers with a neatly cut edge, the poet's carnation or *Dianthus barbatus* is simple and elegant in a bouquet. To add a touch of texture and contrast, arrange them with gypsophila. Carnations and roses are all you need to create a very elegant bouquet.

How do you maintain it?

Carnations with small flowers last longer than those with large flowers. Shorten the stems with a knife and remove any leaves that may be soaking in water. Avoid exposing them to the sun, and don't keep them close to fruit.

PETALS

The flowers of the carnation exhale a delicious scent sometimes reminiscent of cloves.

LEAVES

Its very fine gray-green evergreen foliage grows from a woody base.

COLORS

Green, purple, red, yellow, orange, salmon, white: the carnation offers a wide range of intense colors. Some species are even bicolor.

STEM

The carnation is said to be multifloral because each stem produces a bouquet.

JAPANESE IKEBANA

For thousands of years, the Japanese have practiced the art of floral composition: ikebana, which means "to bring flowers to life." Each flower has its own meaning.

CHRYSANTHEMUM

The chrysanthemum, or *kiku* in Japanese, is the imperial emblem. The flower is also a symbol of longevity. It's used in autumn ikebana compositions. At the Yushima Tenman-gû Shrine in Tokyo, the Chrysanthemum Festival takes place every year in November.

NARCISSUS

The narcissus, called *suisen* in Japanese, is omnipresent in New Year's floral compositions in Japan. This yellow and white flower symbolizes purity and dignity. It's one of the only flowers to bloom in the depths of winter. It evokes the awakening of spring. In Asia, the narcissus is considered a lucky flower.

MAGNOLIA STELLATA

The *Magnolia stellata* owes its name to its white or pinkish star-shaped flowers. Native to Japan, this flower, which grows in spring, is a mark of sincerity in a floral composition.

LILY

The lily is renowned for the intensity of its scent. In an ikebana, the flower, elegant in its whiteness, represents fertility and purity. There are several species of lily in Japan, some of which grow wild.

CAMELLIA JAPONICA

Camellia japonica is the flower that heralds spring. It has become one of the traditional subjects of artistic expression in drawing, painting, poetry, or ikebana. The Japanese also use it in chabana, a floral arrangement used in the tea ceremony.

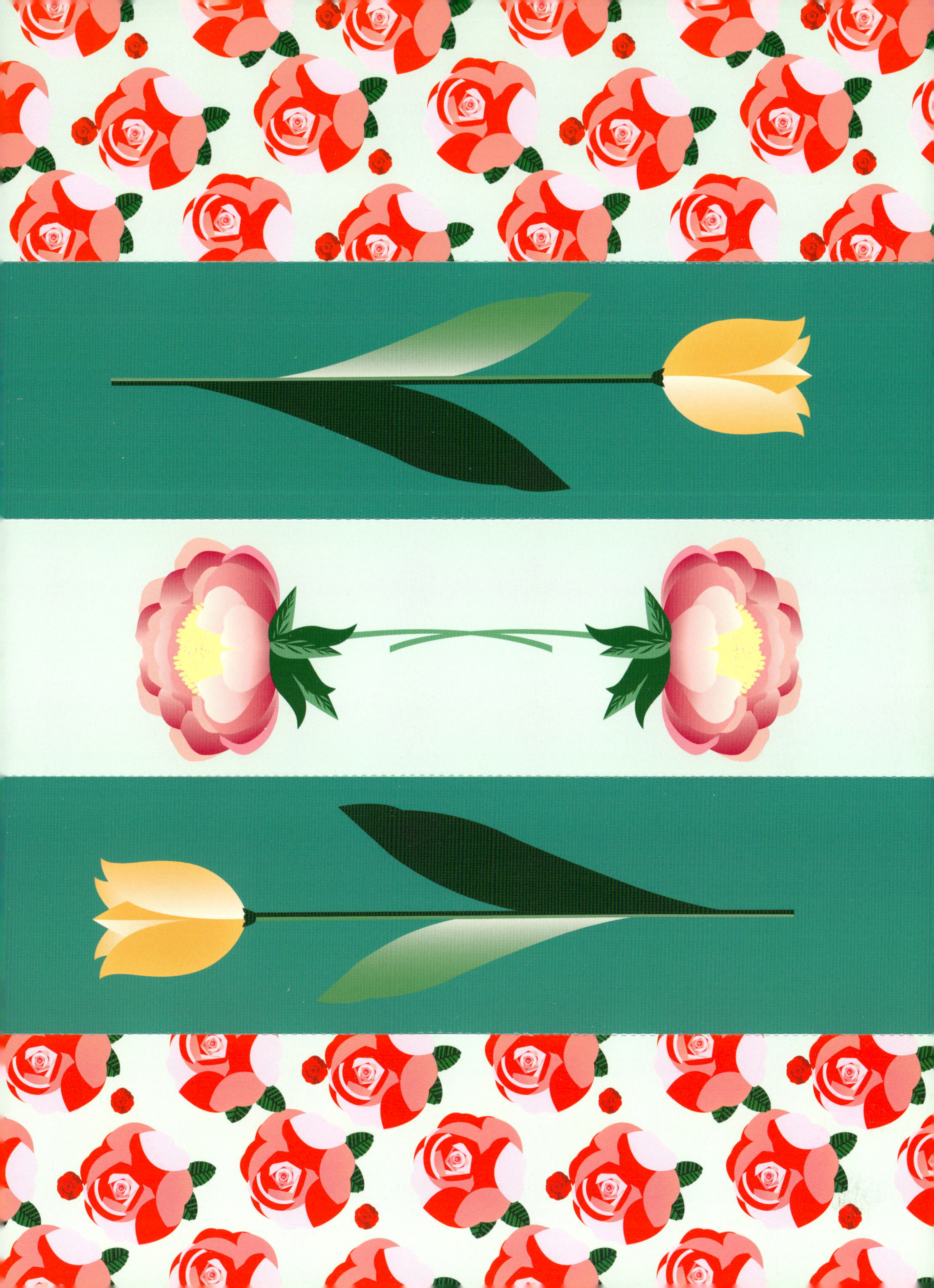

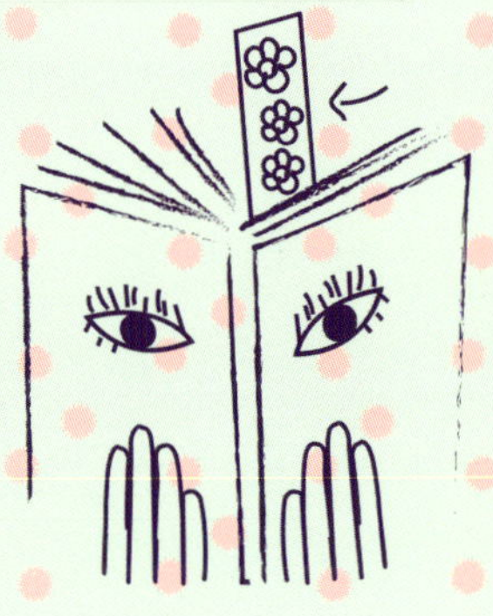

FLORIST

The Art of the Bouquet

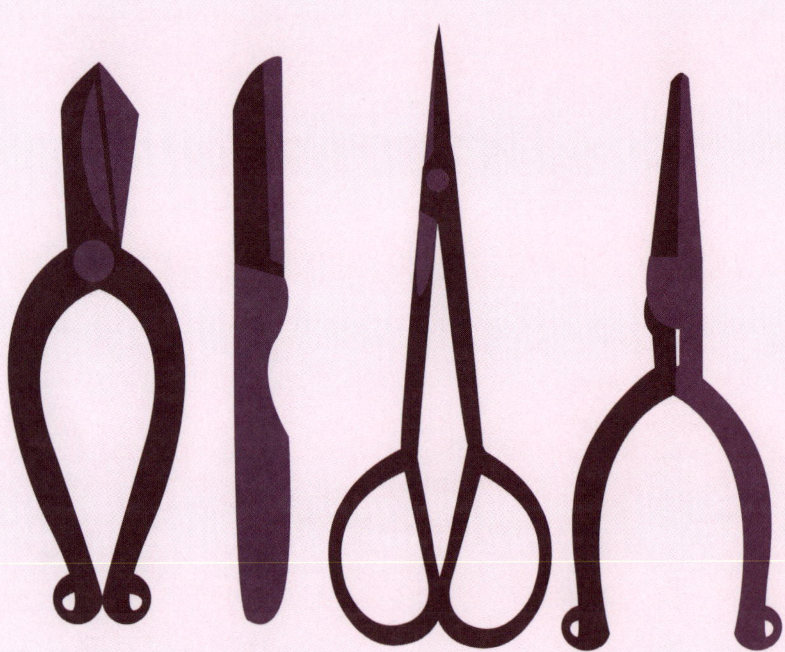

In Egyptian times, floral arrangements were already found in tombs and carved stone reliefs. The Greeks and Romans also used flower arrangements to honor their athletes. Although floral art has been practiced for thousands of years, the flower trade is more recent. The word "florist" appeared in the seventeenth century and referred to a specialist involved in growing and perfecting new varieties of flowers. It was not until the end of the nineteenth century that it was used to refer to a cut-flower merchant.

Early in the morning, he goes to the market to stock up on flowers, plants, and shrubs. Back at the shop, he stores them in ideal conditions of temperature and light. As a true aesthete, the florist knows how to marry the different species, shapes, and colors of flowers. Registered since 1986 in the repertoire of trades, he is considered a true craftsman, handling scissors with dexterity to make floral compositions. Every October 5, we celebrate Sainte-Fleur. This event opens the beginning of the Côte d'Azur flower production season. The blessing of this festival was first celebrated in Nice in the Sainte-Réparate cathedral, near the famous flower market, cours Saleya. As the saying goes, "A bouquet for Sainte-Fleur, all-year-round happiness."

SECATEURS

Available in different sizes, secateurs can be used to cut hard, thick, and woody branches, such as mimosa or rose branches.

KNIFE

A knife is the florist's indispensable accessory. It's used to cut the stems of flowers and to get rid of unwanted leaves.

SCISSORS

With large-eared (bonsai) scissors, the florist cuts fine stems or delicately removes small flowers from bouquets.

BENDING PLIERS

A must in floral art, bending pliers allow the florist to work the decorative metal wires and give them the desired shape.

Bride's Bouquet

Celebrating one's marriage with a bouquet of flowers in hand is an ancient tradition. In those days, they were not flowers, but aromatic herbs. Chives or thyme were supposed to chase away evil spirits and release their sweet aroma, at a time when hygiene sometimes left something to be desired. The bouquet could also contain aphrodisiac herbs. In the Middle Ages, this custom was brought back by the Crusaders, and since weddings were celebrated in spring, orange blossom made up most bouquets. Often white, the flowers symbolize purity. Once the ceremony ended, tradition dictated that the composition was placed on a velvet cushion inside a glass globe to keep it intact for the rest of the couple's life.

THROWING THE BRIDE'S BOUQUET

In the sixteenth century, men had fun running after the bride to try to grab her bouquet, since it was synonymous with happiness; later, throwing the bouquet toward the single women of the wedding party became popular. Today, at the end of the ceremony, the bride throws the bouquet over her shoulder. It's said that the one who catches it will be the next to get married.

MAKE A BOUQUET OF FLOWERY CONFETTI

MATERIALS

- Hole punch
- Origami paper—use the paper from this book
- Sticker
- Raffia

HOW TO

Punch the paper to make as much confetti as possible. Cut the origami paper into squares of varying sizes, depending on the size of the cone you want. Then cut each square diagonally to make triangles. One by one, roll the origami paper triangles on themselves to form a cone. Keep it in place with a sticker. Bind the base of the cone by stapling a sprig of raffia to it.

FLORAL CENTERPIECE

MATERIALS

- 1 block of hydrophilic foam (4.5 x 4 x 3 inches)
- Adhesive tape
- 1 roll of crystal paper
- 5 bear grass stems
- 4 pins
- 15 shallon leaves
- Secateurs
- 2 white hydrangea heads
- 8 red anemones

HOW TO

Soak your foam block in water. Wrap the foam block with crystal paper and tape it down so that the water cannot run off.

Slip shallon leaves around the foam collar into the adhesive tape. Weave five bear grass stems together and secure the ends around the foam with the pins.

Start by inserting the hydrangea flowers into the foam.

Cut the stems of the anemones at an angle with secateurs to allow the water to rise and your flowers to hydrate. Finish dressing the foam by inserting your anemones among the hydrangea flowers.

RECIPE

ORANGE BLOSSOM PANCAKES

INGREDIENTS

- 2½ cups flour
- 2 teaspoons baking soda
- 4 tablespoons sugar
- 4 tablespoons salted butter
- 2 cups milk
- 2 eggs
- ⅓ cup orange blossom water

Mix the flour, baking soda, and sugar. Melt the salted butter in milk over low heat. Beat the eggs with a fork and add to the mixture. Add the orange blossom water to the mixture.

Leave the mixture to rest for thirty minutes in the refrigerator. Decorate the pancakes with a few corn-flower and pansy petals.

WHO'S WHO

HYDRANGEA, BALL FLOWER

What is it?

The hydrangea belongs to the Hydrangea family, which comes from the Latin *hydro* (water) and the Greek *aggos* (vase), due to the shape of its large ball-shaped flowers, reminiscent of ancient water jugs. Originally from Asia, where the plant is called the flower of the eight immortals, it was introduced to France in the eighteenth century by the French navigator and naturalist Philibert Commerson. According to a legend, the name "hydrangea" is a tribute to Hortense, his mistress who secretly accompanied him on this expedition. Following the Fukushima disaster in Japan in 2011, the hydrangea became the symbol of an antinuclear movement: the Hydrangea Revolution. There are now nearly seventy species in Southeast Asia and America, but especially in East Asia.

What is its symbolism?

The hydrangea symbolizes gratitude, grace, and beauty. With its generous round shape and multitude of small flowers, it also evokes abundance and expresses generous and fulfilled feelings. This flower is emblematic of filial love.

How does it fit in a bouquet?

The hydrangea goes very well with all the flowers of its season! Rose, lisianthus, and gypsophila are particularly well suited. Dried and arranged in bunches, it's beautiful. To do so, leave its head up and its stem in 2 inches of water.

How do you maintain it?

Using secateurs, cut the stems at an angle and split them in half. If the petals wilt, plunge their entire head into the water for thirty minutes. Hydrangeas love water and do not like heat and drafts. It's best to water them a little every day with a mister.

FLOWERS

Ball-shaped and composed of multiple flowers arranged in spherical corymbs, the heads can measure up to 10 inches in diameter.

LEAVES

Green sometimes tinged with purple, they are oval and serrated.

STEM

The height of this bushy shrub varies from 16 inches to 6½ feet depending on the variety.

COLORS

Its color changes with the seasons. In spring, it's red, pink, purple, white, green, and blue; then, it turns green, red, and brown in autumn. In acidic soil, pink hydrangea can turn blue.

FLORA-COUTURE

Flowers are an inexhaustible source of inspiration for fashion designers. Everyone has a preference.

COCO CHANEL AND THE CAMELLIA

To the question "What do you have for breakfast?", Gabrielle Chanel once replied, "A camellia." At the age of thirteen, the young woman developed a passion for this flower—native to Asia—during a theatrical performance of *The Lady of the Camellias*, starring Sarah Bernhardt. Her great love of the time, the English polo player Boy Capel, covered her with bouquets. In 1923, the seamstress revived the fashion for the white camellia worn in buttonholes by dandies at the beginning of the twentieth century. This delicate flower was also pinned on the bodices of her muslin dresses and became the brand's signature: the double C logo evokes the shape of its petals.

CHRISTIAN DIOR AND THE LILY OF THE VALLEY

"After women, flowers are the most divine creations," said Christian Dior. They reminded him of the scent of the Norman garden of his childhood in Granville. Like the impressionist painters, Dior designed his collections surrounded by flowers. In 1947, the Corolle line reflected his unconditional love for women and horticulture. His favorite flower was the lily of the valley, a sprig of which he wore in his buttonhole. He also hid some in the hems of his garments like a gris-gris. However, his dream was to capture the aroma of these bunches of bells. Thanks to his master perfumer's talents, he did just that with Diorissimo, which has a delicate scent of lily of the valley.

YVES SAINT LAURENT AND THE BOUGAINVILLEA

Throughout his career, Yves Saint Laurent never ceased to adorn his creations with flowers, be they field, garden, or even exotic flowers. His capes embroidered with bougainvillea—named after Captain Louis-Antoine de Bougainville, who took part in its discovery in the eighteenth century—evoke lush Moroccan gardens. In 1980, the couturier and his companion Pierre Bergé acquired the Majorelle garden in Marrakech and increased the number of species from 135 to 300. The exotic plants in this enchanting garden became a real muse for him. Yves Saint Laurent would even go so far as to affirm that its shimmering colors filled his dreams.

FLORICULTURE

The Slow-Flower Trend

Planting, growing, cutting or digging up, and then selling—that's what floriculture is all about. The business may be specialized in a family of flowers or in different varieties.

In France, most flower farms are located in South France, Ile-de-France, and Brittany. Since the 1970s, globalization has not spared the flower market; today, 80% of cut flowers sold in France come from abroad. Kenya, for example, is the leading exporter of roses, with large farms set up around Lake Naivasha. This tropical cultivation of flowers contributes to drying up the water table in a country where water is a scarce commodity. In recent years, floriculturists have expressed the wish to work in a sustainable way and to rehabilitate local flower varieties by adhering to the principle of the slow flower initiated in England.

CUSTOMIZE YOUR GARDENING NOTEBOOK WITH ORIGAMI PAPER

MATERIALS

- 1 notebook in A5 format
- 2 sheets of origami paper
- White glue

HOW TO

Lay the notebook flat on the sheet of origami paper. Leave a margin of a half inch all around and cut out. Glue the origami paper on the notebook and let it dry. Cut the four corners and a small triangle at the fold of the notebook. Fold the excess paper inside the cover.

TULIP

The size of the bulb indicates the beauty of the flower. Horticultural tulip bulbs have an average size of 4–5 inches in diameter. To obtain a beautiful spring bloom, the tulip bulbs are planted between September and December at a depth of about twice the height of the bulb. It's recommended to space them about 4 inches apart.

DAHLIA

Depending on the variety, this flower native to Mexico blooms in July or August. The tubers are planted between April and May at the waning moon after the last frosts. Space them 2–3 feet apart for large species and 11–20 inches apart for dwarf varieties. Dahlias flower best and longest in the sun.

COSMOS

This annual flower is one of the easiest to grow. Sunshine and well-drained soil are its only requirements. While it's possible to plant them as early as March, it's best to plant them in April or May, as soon as the soil has warmed up, in rows 12–16 inches apart. Flowering starts in June or July and continues until October.

ART NOUVEAU

Ode to Nature

In 1900, architect Hector Guimard was commissioned to decorate the entrances to the Paris metro. He exclaimed: "Nothing is invented; all shapes are already created in nature." Just like the Arts & Crafts movement born in England, art nouveau opposed the industrial era with an inspiring and harmonious nature. The ornamental repertoire from the animal, plant, and mineral kingdoms was a source of inspiration for artists. Floral motifs were reproduced ad infinitum on fabrics, wallpaper, bindings, posters, furniture, and jewelry in a new style. Like true botanists, the artists of the time relied on the discoveries of modern science. In addition to the direct observation of animal and plant forms, the number of collections increased. In 1896, artist Eugène Grasset, who was passionate about horticulture, published *La Plante et Ses Applications Ornementales* (*The Plant and Its Ornamental Applications*). This work featured seventy-two color plates showing the use of plant ornaments in the various fields of the decorative arts.

FLOWER WOMAN

Émile Gallé, another figure of art nouveau, refused to simply imitate nature, "a reservoir of life and not a fixed painting." Artists at the beginning of the twentieth century made Mother Nature undergo metamorphoses, opting for provocative lines and forms: stems and leaves intermingled in extraordinary volutes. The flower was not considered as a still life, but it followed the curves of the piece of furniture and sprang from the walls: "From a gourd comes a bookcase, from a thistle a desk, from a water lily a ballroom," wrote art critic Robert de la Sizeranne. With the discovery of Japanese art, the flora unfolded with refinement. Iris, daffodils, and sunflowers were artists' favorite flowers. These compositions, all in arabesques, "naturally" evoked the woman. Illustrator Alphonse Mucha became famous thanks to his posters representing women with long wavy hair, surrounded by flowers.

RECIPE

ZUCCHINI FLOWER FRITTERS

INGREDIENTS

- 2 dozen zucchini flowers
- 2 cups flour
- 3 eggs
- ½ packet yeast
- 1 large glass of milk
- 1 bunch of parsley
- 2 cups olive oil
- Salt and pepper

Prepare the fritter dough with flour, eggs, milk, a tablespoon of oil, and yeast. Add a little milk if it's thick, or flour if it's too liquid. Mix the preparation vigorously and let it rest.

Add the finely chopped parsley, salt, and pepper and mix again.

Dip the zucchini flowers in the dough and immerse the fritters in very hot oil. Brown them on both sides.

Place each fritter on absorbent paper to remove excess oil. Eat them immediately, while they are hot.

RECIPE

ACACIA FLOWER FRITTERS

INGREDIENTS

- About 15 clusters of acacia flowers
- ½ cup flour
- 1 egg
- ½ cup milk
- ⅓ cup beer
- 2 tablespoons brown sugar
- 1 pinch of salt
- 1 vanilla stalk
- Frying oil
- Confectioners' sugar

Mix the flour, sugar, salt, and egg. Add gradually, mixing in the milk. Incorporate the beer and then the seeds of the vanilla stalk. Rest for one to two hours in the refrigerator.

Heat the frying oil in a frying pan. Dip each bunch of flowers into the dough and dip the fritters in the oil for a few seconds. Brown them on both sides.

Place each fritter on absorbent paper to remove excess oil. Sprinkle with confectioners' sugar and enjoy immediately.

WHO'S WHO

THE CAMELLIA, ASIAN FLOWER

What is it?

In ancient times, the emperors of China cultivated this flower in their gardens, and its blooms were sacred. It appeared in Europe in the eighteenth century as a result of a deception. The Chinese sold *Camellia japonica*, the ornamental variety, to the East India Company instead of *Camellia sinensis* plants, used for tea. This is how the first camellias arrived in London, much to the disappointment of the English, who wanted to establish tea plantations in their colonies. Botanist Charles Linné named this flower in homage of the Jesuit botanist Camellus, whose real name was Georges Joseph Kamel. In France, Empress Josephine de Beauharnais had camellias planted in the gardens of Malmaison.

What is its symbolism?

The camellia symbolizes longevity, fidelity, and happiness. In Japan, the message delivered varies according to its color: red embodies love; yellow expresses lack of love; white represents waiting.

How does it fit in a bouquet?

Easy to mix with other flowers, the camellia blends perfectly with anemone and pieris, commonly called andromeda and recognizable by its white flower clusters. You can also add pittosporum leaves and a few flowers of *Skimmia japonica* for a bouquet that is as fragrant as you would wish.

How do you maintain it?

The camellia is one of the hardiest cut flowers, since it lasts almost a month. It likes cool, damp places. Before putting the flowers in a vase, split the stem about 1½–2 inches and add sugar to the water.

PETALS

Fleshy, they are plain or bicolor. They can also be striped, lined, spotted, speckled, or subtly powdered.

LEAVES

In Japan, the camellia is called *tsubaki*, which means "tree with shiny leaves."

STAMENS

More or less visible depending on the variety, they can be shaped like a crown, a tuft, or a brush.

COLORS

The camellia flower comes in a multitude of shades, ranging from white, yellow, and pink to red and purple.

MAKE A FLORAL TABLEAU

Give a second life to your bouquets by making a floral tableau to resemble a herbarium.

MATERIALS

- Cardboard sheets
- Thick sheets of art paper
- Medium-sized (½ inch thick) wooden boards
- White glue
- A fine brush
- A pair of tweezers
- A glass frame
- An assortment of flowers: gypsophila, roses, black-eyed susan, daisies, hydrangea

When their petals are not too fragile, almost all flowers lend themselves to the creation of a floral painting.

DRYING THE FLOWERS

Dry your flowers immediately after picking, before they wilt. Be careful not to use wet flowers since they may wilt. If you don't have a flower press, it's possible to make your own very easily. Stack (in order) a ½-inch-thick wooden board, a piece of cardboard, a sheet of art paper, and your flowers. Repeat this operation four to five times, finishing with a board. Tighten the flower press with two ratchet straps or, failing that, place a weight on it. Wait between one and three weeks, making sure to renew the sheets of paper from time to time if they are loaded with moisture.

CREATE THE TABLEAU

On a slightly thick sheet of paper, arrange your composition. Place the petals with tweezers.

Photograph your composition to keep it in mind, then glue the flowers one by one by applying a point of glue with a fine brush. Once your composition is finished, place it in the chosen frame. Avoid exposing your creation to direct light, since the colors of the petals will fade.

FRAGRANCE

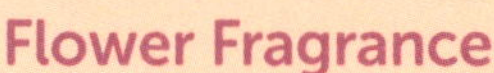

Flower Fragrance

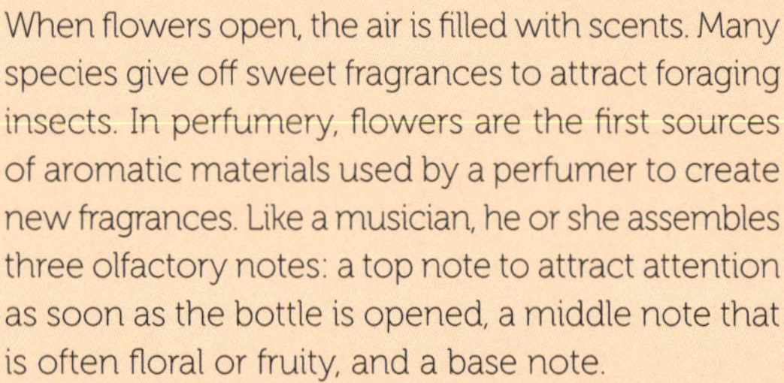

When flowers open, the air is filled with scents. Many species give off sweet fragrances to attract foraging insects. In perfumery, flowers are the first sources of aromatic materials used by a perfumer to create new fragrances. Like a musician, he or she assembles three olfactory notes: a top note to attract attention as soon as the bottle is opened, a middle note that is often floral or fruity, and a base note.

In his perfume barrel, the composer/perfumer has several thousand different raw materials at his disposal, of which only 400 to 500 are of natural origin; the rest are synthetic bodies. With the Industrial Revolution, thanks to advances in chemistry, the so-called silent flowers—lilac, lily of the valley, violet, hyacinth, honeysuckle—were added to perfume. Perfume was no longer just a mixture of natural ingredients, of animal or vegetable origin; it became an artistic and abstract construction of olfactory forms.

CONCOCT SCENTED WATER FOR YOUR HOME

INGREDIENTS

- 1 to 3 cups of water
- A dozen or so rose, orchid, or lily petals
- 1 tablespoon water/rose hydrolyte
- 1 tablespoon grapefruit seed extract

HOW TO

Put all the ingredients in a saucepan and heat over low heat. Let simmer for fifteen minutes, stirring frequently. Transfer the scented water to previously sterilized bottles.

Decorate your bottle of scented water with one of the beautiful labels proposed in this book.

IRIS

Although iris flowers sometimes have delicious scents, the essence of the plant is obtained from the rhizome—known as iris butter because it freezes at room temperature. Its yield is extremely low, since it takes 16 tons of flowers to obtain 2 pounds of absolue, the essence of perfume. This makes it one of the most expensive materials in perfumery: about 15,000 euros per pound!

TUBEROSE

Native to Mexico, tuberose is a white flower much coveted in perfumery, with a scent that is both refined and heady. It produces a fragrant substance forty-eight hours after picking. During the Renaissance, young girls were forbidden to walk in tuberose fields for fear that the erotic scent of the flowers would make them lose their heads.

JASMINE

It's one of the perfumers' favorite flowers. It has been used in Chanel N°5 since 1921. Of the 200 existing varieties, only two are used in perfumery: sambac jasmine and Spanish jasmine (grandiflorum). Undetectable during the day, the flower is fragrant at nightfall. About 1,500 pounds of jasmine flowers, hand-picked at dawn, are necessary to produce 2 pounds of absolue. Introduced in Grasse in the sixteenth century, very little production remains. The cultivated area of jasmine is confined to a few acres and almost exclusively reserved for the house of Chanel.

DANDYISM
The Floral Boutonniere

In the eighteenth century, men's garments no longer closed across the chest: this was the birth of French-style dressing. The buttonhole on the lapel was used only for ornamental purposes. Aristocrats put their military decoration in it, while artists preferred to put a flower in it.

THE WRITERS' DARLING?

Dandies adopted the custom of adorning their buttonholes in the nineteenth century, and wearing a flower in the buttonhole became a sign of elegance. This fancy ornament was reserved for social functions, since official events did not allow this accessory, which was considered a little too arty. The black jacket with tails and silk lapels, with matching shirt, tie, and waistcoat, was then de rigueur in the evening. Men usually wore a white flower: a carnation, camellia, or gardenia. The writer Barbery d'Aurevilly proclaimed himself a Knight of the Order of Spring and declared that he would sacrifice a rose every evening in his buttonhole. Oscar Wilde established the green carnation as a symbol of homosexual love. For the Irish writer and his companion Lord Alfred Douglas, this seductive flower became the code of recognition for those who had the courage of their convictions.

THE VASE BUTTONHOLE: ENGLISH CHIC

In England, it was fashionable to arrange boutonniere flowers in small gold or silver vases to keep them fresh. This was the essential accessory for Agatha Christie's hero, Hercule Poirot.

MAKE A FLORAL BOUTTONIERE

MATERIALS

- Carnation, camellia, lily of the valley, peony
- Pair of bonsai scissors
- Floral adhesive
- Ribbon or raffia
- Buttonhole support or safety pin

HOW TO

Cut the stems to 4 inches and remove the leaves. Form a bouquet and tie the stems together with floral tape. Adjust the length of the stems. Attach the bouquet to the buttonhole support with floral tape. Cover with a ribbon or a piece of raffia to hide the fastening. You have the elegance of bygone days!

You can favor one flower in particular or create your boutoniere with up to three assorted flowers.

FLORAL DRINKS

FLOWER PIMP MY COLLINS

INGREDIENTS

- 3 tablespoons gin
- 1½ tablespoons elderflower liqueur
- 1½ tablespoons lemon juice
- 5 tablespoons sparkling water

Pour the gin, lemon, and liqueur into a large glass. Top it off with ice. Stir with a spoon and complete with sparkling water.

Use the coasters from this book to decorate your table.

MEXICO SUNSHINE

INGREDIENTS

- 3 tablespoons tequila
- 1½ tablespoons cointreau
- 4 tablespoons passion fruit juice
- 4 tablespoons grapefruit juice
- 4 drops of ylang-ylang floral water

Mix the ingredients in a shaker or blender, serve in a large tumbler filled with ice, and decorate with grapefruit zest and a strawberry cut into a fan shape.

Use the coasters from this book to decorate your table.

WHO'S WHO

THE LILY, KING OF FLOWERS

What is it?

If the rose is the queen of flowers, the lily is the king! With its majestic flowers and heady scent, this bulbous plant has always aroused admiration. In Greek mythology, the lily is associated with the goddess Hera, symbol of motherhood. As she suckled Heracles, a drop of milk fell to the earth, giving birth to a white lily. Out of jealousy, Aphrodite sullied the purity of this flower by adding yellow stamens. Brought from the East by the Crusaders, the lily came to represent the purity of the Virgin Mary. It became the symbol of France and French royalty from the eleventh century until the Revolution.

What is its symbolism?

In the time of the Greeks and Romans, brides received a crown of lilies as a sign of virginity. Red proclaims passion, pink represents affection and tenderness, yellow represents friendship and cheerfulness, and orange means desire.

How does it fit in a bouquet?

Its generous and imposing flower makes it possible to make majestic bouquets. The lily can be combined with roses, delphiniums, hellebores, blue asters, or red angelica. In a large colored vase, a simple stem of three to five buds that will open in turn is enough to perfume an entire room.

How do you maintain it?

The pollen on lily stamens leaves indelible stains, especially on fabrics. It's therefore best to take care not to damage the pistil in the center of the flower. Lily flowers can last longer when the stamens are removed.

STAMENS

The royal lily has six stamens, the male part of the flower.

THE TEPALS

Its large flowers have six tepals (three petals and three identical sepals) which can reach 10 inches in diameter. They can be trumpet, turban, cup, or funnel shaped.

COLORS

It comes in a variety of delightful colors: white, orange, red, yellow, pink, and pale orange, with spotted, speckled, or variegated patterns.

THE ANTHERS

An essential part of the stamen, the anther is suspended from a filament and contains the pollen. It is yellow-orange.

MAKE A DRIED-FLOWER BOUQUET

How do you make flowers immortal? Vintage, natural, and timeless, a bouquet of dried flowers sublimates our interiors.

AIR DRYING

The most common method of drying flowers is to hang them upside down. Start by removing the leaves from the bottom of the stems. Make small bunches of ten to twenty stems and tie them with raffia or string. Spread the leaves and flowers of each bunch well apart so that they don't touch each other. Then hang the bunches upside down by tying them with wire or string, and leave space between each bunch. Also, choose a place away from the light so as not to alter the colors of the petals. Some species, such as hydrangeas, alliums, gypsophila, and delphiniums, dry best in an upright position with the stems immersed in a small amount of water.

IDEAL FLOWERS

Sunflower, blue thistle, delphinium, hydrangea, yarrow, chrysanthemum, dahlia, and gypsophila are the classics of a dry bouquet. Only soft-stemmed flowers are not recommended. For a fragrant bouquet, add sprigs of lavender, mimosa, broom, peonies, and eucalyptus leaves. Poppy capsules and grasses will give the bouquet a country feel. Finally, add a few billy buttons; these yellow pom-pom flowers will brighten up your floral arrangement.

TAKING CARE OF A BOUQUET OF DRIED FLOWERS

If the petals are wrinkled or stunted, simply expose them to steam from a kettle. They will regain their tone. To prevent the flowers from crumbling, use hairspray. And to protect against dust, nothing works better than the air of a hairdryer set to cool.

To give your bouquet of dried flowers an even more natural look, wrap it with the paper that comes with this book. And to display your bouquet, why not use one of the vases from the stationery pages of the book?

POTPOURRI

The Herbarium of Fragrances

MAKE A POTPOURRI

HOW TO

To create your potpourri, let your nose and your creativity do the talking. You can mix petals and flower buds (rose, lavender, jasmine, heliotrope, mimosa, carnation, violet), bark (cinnamon, rosewood, pine), crushed spices (vanilla, ginger, cardamom, nutmeg, coriander, cloves, cinnamon, star anise), aromatic plants (mint, verbena, rosemary, thyme, laurel, eucalyptus), and fruits (orange, apple, kumquat).

To prolong the aroma of your potpourri, add a few drops of essential oils and a fixative, like powdered iris root or incense, benjamin essence, or dried tonka beans. It's advisable to keep the mixture for six weeks in an airtight container that is stirred regularly. The longer the potpourri macerates, the better the fragrance. Your floral mixture can also be used to garnish scented sachets that will perfume your laundry and cupboards.

Make scented sachets and attach a label indicating the aromas.

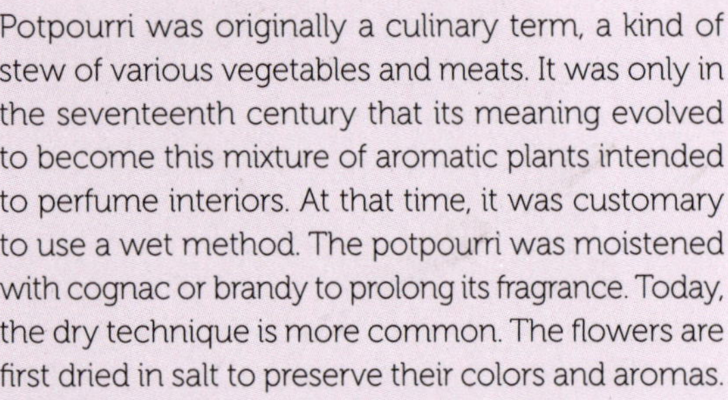

Potpourri was originally a culinary term, a kind of stew of various vegetables and meats. It was only in the seventeenth century that its meaning evolved to become this mixture of aromatic plants intended to perfume interiors. At that time, it was customary to use a wet method. The potpourri was moistened with cognac or brandy to prolong its fragrance. Today, the dry technique is more common. The flowers are first dried in salt to preserve their colors and aromas.

LAVENDER

Lavender, with its powerful, floral, and herbaceous fragrance, is the essential aromatic plant in the composition of a potpourri. It can be used in almost all aromatic mixtures. Its fragrance is known for its relaxing and soothing action. As early as the sixteenth century, it was customary to fill mattresses and pillows with aromatic plants, including lavender, for a good night's sleep.

ROSE

The rose is the star flower of the potpourri. It brings its subtle fragrance and beautiful colors to this decorative mix. In the eighteenth century, at a time when potpourri was very fashionable in England, these preparations were mainly prepared with rose petals. Although all varieties are fragrant, the May rose (*Rosa centifolia*) has an unequaled olfactory richness. Its fragrance is less honeyed than the *Rosa damascena*, grown in Bulgaria and Turkey.

MIMOSA

With its dazzling golden pom-poms, mimosa exhales a soft, powdery scent. Its scent is mysterious and subtle. It's often associated with tuberose, carnation, and rose. In a potpourri, the scent of mimosa gives an impression of balance and comfort.

Scented Gloves

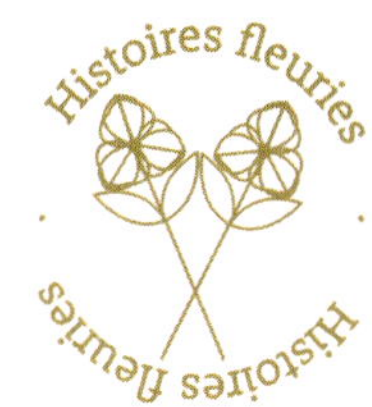

In the noble residences of the sixteenth century, objects of frivolity were perfumed: jewels, fans, and velvet masks, even rare birds in aviaries. Catherine de Medici brought the fashion of perfumed gloves to the Court of Versailles. This accessory above all protected against epidemics, while creating a fragrant halo around the wearer, leaving the memory of his or her passage through a room.

GRASSE, PERFUME CAPITAL

Renowned in the Middle Ages for the quality of its tanneries, Grasse opened up to perfumery at the beginning of the eighteenth century. The exceptional climate of the region makes it possible to grow jasmine, orange, rose, tuberose, and many other plants typical of southern Italy. At that time, the profession of perfumer was associated with that of glovemaker to satisfy the fashion of the moment. The perfumers of Grasse organized themselves into a real corporation. In 1729, they received the official status of glove perfumers, which they kept until the French Revolution.

MANUFACTURE

Making scented gloves was a long and delicate operation. The leather was first colored with vegetable, mineral, or animal pigments. To deodorize them, they were placed in boxes alternating with beds of daffodils, hyacinths, violets, roses, or tuberose and then dried in the sun. This treatment took a minimum of eight days, after which the cut and sewn gloves carried the scent of the flower. On the eve of the Revolution, the profession was affected by heavy taxation on leather and gradually abandoned glove making to focus on perfumery.

FLORAL DRINKS

ROSE OF BOMBAY

INGREDIENTS

- 3 tablespoons gin
- 1½ tablespoons blackcurrant cream
- 1½ tablespoons cranberry juice
- ⅔ tablespoon raspberry jam
- 4 drops of rose water

Mix everything in a shaker, serve in a dry martini glass, and decorate with rose petals and fresh raspberries.

Use the coasters from this book to decorate your table.

RELAXING SMOOTHIE

INGREDIENTS

4 tablespoons mango juice

3 tablespoons banana juice

3 tablespoons milk

3 tablespoons soymilk

1 teaspoon orange blossom water

Mix everything in the shaker, serve with ice cubes, and decorate with borage flowers.

Use the coasters from this book to decorate your table.

THE THISTLE, PRICKLY FLOWER

What is it?

It pricks our fingers! This mountain plant from the artichoke family is easily recognizable by its thorny foliage and blue or purple-pink tubular flowers. The Greeks and Romans used it for medicinal purposes, and pregnant women ate it to have a son! It was also thought to be able to repel evil spirits with its thorns. Since the fifteenth century, the thistle has been the emblem of Scotland in memory of a victory against Viking invaders. Legend has it that the Vikings tried to invade a citadel at night. Having taken off their shoes to approach quietly, they stumbled upon a field of thistles. Their screams of pain alerted the Scottish guards of their arrival.

What is its symbolism?

Even though the thistle is the symbol of austerity, adding a few of these flowers to a bouquet undeniably spices it up!

How does it fit in a bouquet?

The bright color of the thistle means it can be used with many other flowers: blue delphiniums, yellow goldenrod, red anemones, lisianthus, or sea lavender. Thistles also look great in a bouquet of dried flowers.

How do you maintain it?

Thistles are rustic, hardy, low-maintenance flowers. In bunches, they can easily last two weeks. Before immersing them in warm water, cut their stems slightly. To dry them, hang a bouquet upside down in the open air.

FLOWERS

Like artichoke and sagebrush, its florets are united in a capitulum.

BRACTS

They are equipped with rigid spines.

LEAVES

The green leaves are more or less cut out and contrast with its small steel-blue balls.

COLORS

Depending on the species (milk thistle, creeping thistle, or alpine blue thistle), its flower has blue, yellow, white, red, or purple hues.

MAKE A COUNTRY FLOWER BOUQUET

Take advantage of your hikes to pick seasonal flowers and play the florist's apprentice by composing a pretty country bouquet.

PICKING FLOWERS

When picking flowers, try not to damage the plant. Instead of pulling and risking pulling out its roots, cut the stem with secateurs. To avoid twisting the stems or breaking the flower heads, place your collection in a flat-bottomed basket. Limit your choice to two or three colors of flowers. There is also no need to multiply the varieties. Here again, two or three are enough.

CUTTING STEMS

Once you have finished harvesting, shorten the stems by at least 1 inch with a sharp knife, preferably under a trickle of water. By avoiding air penetration, you will facilitate the rise of water in the stem. With the exception of hollow-stemmed flowers, the cut is always beveled. This way, they stand on their tip and there is no risk of the stems sticking to the bottom of the vase. If the stem has nodules, as with carnations, always cut above them to allow water to penetrate more easily. Then remove the leaves at the base of the stems. If you soak them in water, they may rot.

MAKING THE BOUQUET

To form a harmonious sheaf of gleaned flowers, hold a flower in your hand to form the center of the bouquet. Then place the next flowers next to the first, crossing the stems. Rotate the bouquet in your hands a quarter turn, then add more flowers, crossing the stems in the same direction, without squeezing them. To give relief to your bouquet and make it denser, add foliage and grasses. Tie the finished bouquet tightly at the narrowest part of the spray.

And to show off your bouquet, why not use one of the vases from the stationery pages of the book?

DIY

NATURAL PACKAGING MADE OF KRAFT PAPER

1: Begin by positioning your Kraft sheet horizontally.

2: Incline the sheet slightly to the right.

3–4: Press on the fold.

5: Tie the stems with an elastic band and place your bouquet on the paper, so that the elastic band is aligned with the folded edge of the sheet.

6: Wrap the paper around the flowers to make a kind of cone.

7: Fix the paper with a sticker that you will find in this book and bind your composition with a sprig of raffia.

Use the paper from the book to wrap your bouquet of country flowers.

MANDALA

Harmony in a Circle

The word "mandala" comes from Sanskrit and means "circle." In Indian and Tibetan traditions, this diagram, which brings together other geometric forms, has been used for centuries for meditation. The mandala symbolically represents humanity's place in the universe. In Tibet, Buddhists make mandalas with colored sand. No sooner than the sands are finished, they are swept up and collected in a vase, offered to the deities, then poured into a stream as a way of recalling the ephemeral nature of life.

Carl Gustav Jung was one of the first psychiatrists to discover the therapeutic virtues of these drawings. After several years of research, he came to the conclusion that from a psychological point of view, the mandala represented the totality of the person. Harmony and balance are found around the same central point, created by the mandala. Thus, someone who is going through a difficult phase in life can reconnect to its structure by drawing or coloring a mandala. Focusing on this central point would improve concentration and dexterity and bring us back to the present moment. Thanks to the Swiss doctor, the practice has been democratized in the West. Its benefits are now unanimously recognized: refocusing, inner calm, self-knowledge, appeasement.

HOW TO CREATE A MANDALA GARDEN

Start by drawing a map. Identical to a rose window, the mandala garden is organized around a center. The inside of the circle can be divided into other geometric shapes: square, circle, triangle, or spiral. Place a water feataure or a sculpture in the center of the circle.

Once the sketch is finished, mark out the mandala on the ground, making sure to leave paths for easy access to the plants. Mandalas have four doors: each one corresponds to a cardinal point and an element, which allows you to find your way around.

Around the central point, color each area with flowers respecting the four elements: water, fire, air, and earth.

In the north, choose flowers that symbolize water: jasmine, clematis, bindweed, daffodil.

In the south, choose yellow or orange flowers that symbolize fire: marigold, zinnia, sunflower, marigold.

In the east, select plants that symbolize the air: grass, cosmos.

In the west, use root-flowers symbolizing the earth: iris, morning glory.

WILLIAM MORRIS'S

Floral Designs

William Morris began his career as an architect before moving toward drawing and design. Freshly engaged to Jane Burden, the model of his painter friend Dante Gabriel Rossetti, the young man decided to have his house built in the countryside in the middle of an apple orchard. The red-brick house was named Red House. After William Morris moved in, he discovered that he could find no furniture or decorative items to his liking in shops. With the help of his Pre-Raphaelite friends, he decided to make everything himself: wallpaper, drapes, tiles, stained glass.

A COMPOSITION GENIUS

On the strength of his experiments in the Red House, William Morris founded a decorating company called Morris, Marshall, Faulkner & Co. in 1861. He intended to raise the decorative arts to the level of the major arts. The firm quickly prospered as Morris proved to be a genius at composition. Inspired by nature, his wallpaper and upholstery designs surpassed what factories produced. All are hand-printed with wooden stamps.

TULIP WALLPAPER

Fifteen years later, William Morris became the sole proprietor of Morris & Co. and the most sought-after decorator in London. London's elite adored his first chintz—a printed cotton canvas, used in furnishings—with tulips intertwined with willow leaves. This allowed him to perfect his printing techniques and to revive natural dyes. The palette of red, blue, ocher, and soft green was obtained with vegetable pigments. At this time, William Morris and John Ruskin launched the Arts & Crafts movement. Paving the way for art deco, its artists found their inspiration mainly in nature. Flowers such as lilies, honeysuckle, jasmine, or daisy were recurring motifs.

GLOSSARY

A-B

Absolue: Natural concentrate of perfume extracted from a material vegetable—flower, bark, seed, wood, or root

Anther: Part at the top of the cheesecloth containing the pollen seeds

Annual: Refers to plants whose complete vegetative cycle takes place over the course of a year. Sown in the spring, they die in the winter.

Aromatic: A plant whose properties are used in cooking, in perfumery, in cosmetology or in phytotherapy

Bevel: An oblique cut

Bract: Leaf at the base of the flower or inflorescence stalk

Bulb: Underground bulge at the base of a plant stem holding a tiny germ, ready to bloom the following year

C – D – E – F

Calyx: Outer envelope compared to a calyx-shaped vase, consisting of the sepals. It covers the lower part of the corolla of a flower and protects its sex organs.

Concrete: Solid product or semisolid obtained after extraction of some raw materials of vegetable origin—jasmine, rose, narcissus

Collar: Accessory in various textures for the enhancement of a floral work

Corolla: Inner envelope of the flower formed by the petals, often colored or decorative

Corymbs: Inflorescence where the flowers are on the same plan, but where the stalks are of unequal length, like the hydrangea

Cultivar: Name given to a selected plant horticultural and not present at the natural state

Deciduous: Refers to a plant that loses its leaves in autumn

Distillation: A technique of steam distillation to collect the odorous elements, essential oils, contained in certain natural raw materials

Enfleurage: An ancient method of cold extraction of floral products developed in Grasse, using the property that certain fats have of absorbing and retaining odorous principles

Essential oil: Refers to the aromatic and volatile product extracted from plants, by distillation or by expression

Floriculture: Cultivation of flowers and plants

Flower head: Inflorescence form consisting of a receptacle bearing tiny flowers squeezed together against each other and surrounded by bracts

G – H –I – J – K

Globular (flower): Refers to a spherical flower, such as the allium

Glomeruli (flowers in): Inflorescence where the flowers are very tightly packed, carried by short peduncles, and joined in a globular shape, like the mimosa

Herbarium: Collection of plants that are dried to preserve them

Heliotrope: A plant that turns its flowers toward the sun, like the sunflower

Hydrophilic: Absorbs water

Hydrolyte: An aromatic aqueous preparation obtained by distilling water in which a vegetable substance is immersed after separation of the essential oil

Ikebana: Traditional Japanese floral art, governed by a symbolic codification

Inflorescence: The arrangement of flowers on the stem of a plant

Incomplete: A flower that is missing one or more floral parts—petals, stamens, carpals, or sepals

L – M – N – O

Lancer: An elongated, oval plant organ with a point at the end

Male: A flower that contains only male organs, the stamens

Mute: A flower that is fragrant in nature, but from which it's impossible to extract the perfume. This is the case with violet, lily, lilac, peony, gardenia, honeysuckle, lily of the valley.

Node: A bulge on a stem at a branch or at the point of articulation of a leaf

Note: Characteristic of the odor of a raw material or composition. In perfumery, we speak of floral, cypress, amber notes.

Ovary: Part at the bottom of the pistil containing the eggs. After fertilization, the ovaries give the fruit and the eggs.

P – Q – R

Parasol: Parasol-shaped inflorescence whose components are all attached at the same point and then aligned at the same height

Peduncle: Stem bearing a flower; a fruit

Perfume organ: Furniture for storing the various fragrant raw materials

Philter: Magic drink intended to inspire love

Pistil: Female organ of the plants located in the center of a flower, often shaped like a out of a bottle

Plant: Young plant from a sowing, to be transplanted or replanted

Pluriflora: This carries several flowers, like the cherry tree.

Pollen: Pollen-producing male organ of the flower, usually consisting of the fillet and the anther, located between the corolla and the pistil

Potpourri: Fragrant blend of dried flowers and other plants

Raffia: Natural fiber extracted from a palm tree and used to bind or decorate in floristry

Reproduction: Perfumery composition naively re-creating the smell of a raw material

Rhizome: Stem located at ground level or underground, horizontal, resembling a root. It allows the propagation of the flower.

S – T – U – V – W

Scythe: Wide iron blade and sharp, curved into crescent shape. This tool allows the florist to bevel stems and remove rose thorns.

Secateurs: Robust horticultural pruners

Sepal: Vegetative organ often resembling a small leaf and surrounding the flower bud

Simple: A flower with a normal number of petals. When it has more, it's called semidouble or double.

Species: Botanical term defining a particular plant found in its natural state

Spine: Refers to the thorns of roses or cacti

Stem: Herbaceous stem without leaves or twigs, intended to bear only the flower and fruit, such as gladiolus

Stigma: Sticky end of the pistil that receives pollen grains during fecundation

Style: Generally long tube and thin ending with the stigma where pollen enters

Tuber: Name given to a swollen stem or root with the nutrient reserves used for propagation or consumption

Unifloral: Plant that bears only one flower

Variety: Name given to a plant that varies slightly from the typical species

Woody: A vegetal part that has the consistency of wood

FLOWERS EVERYWHERE

Tulip Festival at Keukenhof
Located southwest of Amsterdam, this 79-acre park has seven million flowering bulbs in spring, including 800 different kinds of tulips. In April, on the occasion of the Bloemencorso (the blooming corso), floats decorated with daffodils, tulips, and hyacinths parade along the park.

The International Floralies in Nantes
Every five years since 1956, the Parc des expositions de la Beaujoire in Nantes hosts the Floralies internationales, an event that attracts flower lovers from all over the world.

Nice Carnival
The Nice carnival takes place every winter in February. Costumed models parade on floats decorated with flowers and throw a shower of flowers to the public. The battle of flowers is a unique spectacle for which the French Riviera is famous.

The Time of Flowers in Girona
During this floral event, the city of Girona in Spain adorns its streets and monuments with the most-beautiful flowers.

La Batalla de Flores in Valencia
Since 1891, after the parade of floral floats, the public throws flowers at the people on the floats, who try to protect themselves with a tennis racket.

The Infiorata in Genzano
Since the eighteenth century, the main street of the small town of Genzano in Italy has been covered with a carpet of flower petals on Corpus Christi, sixty days after Easter.

The Chelsea Flower Show in London
Organized by the Royal Horticultural Society (RHS), this event, which dates back more than a century, is one of the most beautiful horticultural festivals in Europe. It features incredible and colorful floral arrangements and flower constructions.

The Carpet of Flowers in Brussels
Every two years on the weekend of August 15, the floor of the famous Grand-Place in Brussels is covered with a 250-by-80-foot carpet of flowers—begonias, dahlias, grasses, and bark. A hundred volunteers assemble the carpet in less than eight hours.

Madeira Flower Festival
This island, favorable to flowers thanks to its subtropical climate, hosts the Spring Flower Festival. On the eve of the parade, the children build a symbolic "Wall of Hope" in flowers. The next day, floats decorated with thousands of flowers invade Funchal, the capital of the Portuguese island.

The Feria de las Flores in Medellín
In Colombia, flowers are in the spotlight during this festival, considered the most important in the city since 1957. The farmers of the region, called silleteros, parade carrying on their backs wooden constructions decorated with all kinds of flowers. Some of them weigh up to 130 pounds!

Patios Festival in Cordoba
The city of Cordoba in Andalusia celebrates its annual Patios Festival in May, a famous tradition included in the intangible cultural heritage by UNESCO. On this occasion, the inhabitants decorate the whitewashed walls of their courtyards with geraniums, carnations, and jasmine.

THE AUTHORS

Sara Princé

Illustrator and art director Sara Princé's graphic writing crosses the fields of culture, fashion, and design, placing timeless yet highly fashionable signs. Her graphic language joyfully mixes illustrations, poetry of forms, and chromatic research.

"I designed this book as a flowery banquet where artists, family, and friends are invited to tastefully cultivate beautiful flowers, love of color, paper, art, and pattern. It's a floral pop festival that smells of childhood and its memories tinged with soap flowers, fields of sunflowers, roses, thistles from the Cevennes, and festive Liberty blouses. I imagined it colored like the huge brews of dahlias from my grandmother's garden and lightly scented with the dandy charm of a poetic and literary spleen; joyful like a 1970s bohemian skirt or lush like English wallpaper. This book is an invitation to creation: picking flowers, observing them, composing bouquets, imagining motifs, decorative objects, gifts, writing flowery cards. A deep breath of fresh air to create Flower Power!"

Sandrine Tournigand

Sandrine Tournigand is a freelance journalist who works for several magazines—fashion, society, lifestyle, culture, theater, economy . . . her interests are many and varied. In another life, her dream would have been to become an artisan florist. Moreover, if she could reincarnate, it would be as a freesia for the subtle perfume of its flowers.

"To write this book, flowers have been my muses, my confidants: they have revealed their hidden messages, their magical powers, their travels, their fragrance, their tradition, and their expression. Their stories have guided my research, taking me all over the globe. With their prodigious variety of shapes and colors, flowers brighten the world and our lives."

Other Schiffer Books on Related Subjects:

Blooming Paper, Laura Reed,
ISBN 978-0-7643-6208-8

Floral Doodling Handbook, Julie Adore,
ISBN 978-0-7643-6183-8

Paper Joy for Every Room, Laure Farion,
ISBN 978-0-7643-6055-8

Originally published as *Flower Feel Good: La fleur, un art de vivre qui fait du bien!* by Sara Princé and Sandrine Tournigand, ©2019, Editions Rustica, Paris
Translated from the French by Simulingua, Inc.

Library of Congress Control Number: 2021946202

Photos & styling: Roland Krieg
Illustrations : Sara Princé
Type set in Museo/Museo Rounded

ISBN: 978-0-7643-6310-8
Printed in India
Published by Schiffer Publishing, Ltd.
4880 Lower Valley Road
Atglen, PA 19310
Phone: (610) 593-1777; Fax: (610) 593-2002
Email: Info@schifferbooks.com
Web: www.schifferbooks.com